Jock Marshall and Russell Drysdale *Journey Among Men*

Billy the Lurk was restrained from drinking intoxicating liquor for three months.

Jock Marshall &
Russell Drysdale

Journey Among MEN

Sun Books
Melbourne

Sun Books Pty Ltd, South Melbourne, Victoria 3205, Australia

First published by Hodder & Stoughton 1962
Published in Sun Books 1966
Reprinted 1967 (twice), 1968, 1972, 1973, 1975

Text © Jock Marshall and Russell Drysdale 1962
Illustrations © Russell Drysdale 1962

National Library of Australia
cataloguing in publication data

Marshall, Alan John, 1911-1967.
  Journey among men [by] Jock Marshall and Russell Drysdale –
  South Melbourne, Vic.: Sun Books, 1966
  ISBN 0 7251 0017 6.

1. Australia – description and travel. I. Drysdale, Sir George Russell
  1912 –   , joint author.
  II. Title.

919.4

Printed in Hong Kong

For Bon and Janey
who were kind enough to stay at home

ACKNOWLEDGEMENTS

The authors are indebted to the editors of *The Observer*, *The Geographical Magazine*, *The Listener*, *Endeavour* and *Scientific American* for permission to republish certain passages in the present work. Messrs Angus & Robertson Ltd, Sydney, have allowed us to quote parts of A. B. Paterson's *The Man from Snowy River* and *Clancy of the Overflow*. The brief quotation relating to a man's Matilda is taken from J. P. Bourke's *Off the Blue Bush*, published by Tyrrell's Ltd, Sydney, to whom further thanks are due.

'It's nothing,' said The Smiler, 'but did you hear about the local sin-shifter and Micky O'Flaherty's black eye?'

I

This is a story of a journey among men – 'characters' such as Harmonious Harry, Brandy John, The Tropical Frog, and Rob Moody who keeps the pub at Hall's Creek out near the Territory border. And behind them stand a group from the past – the outlaws Sandemara or 'Pigeon', Captain, Demon and Long Franky, whose exploits still make conversation around the campfires of the Australian north-west.

We heard about these as we travelled up the north-western coast collecting zoological specimens. Soon we found ourselves as much interested in people as in animals. At Port Hedland there was an official notice on the pub wall that Whispering Smith (without inverted commas or further identification) had taken out an order restraining Billy the Lurk from drinking intoxicating liquor for a period of three months.

We were pleased with this notice and asked The Smiler, a neighbouring drinker, what it was about.

'It's nothing,' he said. 'Merely that Whispering Smith, the manager of one of the sheep stations near here, has put Billy the Lurk – the cook – under the Dog Act.

'That's why,' he repeated. 'But did you hear about the local sin-shifter and Micky O'Flaherty's black eye?'

We had not heard about O'Flaherty's black eye, but it was obvious that we were going to. O'Flaherty, it seems, was walking down the main drag of Port Hedland when the Father O'Dooley accosted him.

'And how did you get that black eye, Michael O'Flaherty,' he demanded.

Mick explained that he'd had it from Jimmy O'Rourke, in a foight.

'Shame on you, Michael,' said the good Father, 'shame on you for fightin', and double shame on you for lettin' a little cock-sparrow like Jimmy O'Rourke blacken your eye.'

Mick was stung by the second criticism.

'It was what he had in his hand, Father, that did the damage – and it was an axe handle that he had in his hand.'

The Father O'Dooley considered the matter.

'And what did you have in *your* hand, Michael O'Flaherty?' he asked.

And Mick replied: 'I had Mrs O'Rourke's waist in me hand, Father – a beautiful thing in itself but complately useless in a foight!'

2

After years of exile in Europe it was good to be back among the cold beer and red dust on the fringe of the desert. Not that the Australian deserts are really deserts in the traditional sense. You do not see mile after mile of soft undulating sand, enlivened every now and then by a shady oasis of date palms, and all that. The Australian desert is quite different. Not a single palm tree did we see, nor very little sand either, for that matter. We could travel at a leisurely pace in the spring-time, and it was generally not too uncomfortably hot. During most nights we were glad to crawl into our sleeping bags.

This part of Australia is an old, red, rigid land. It is a land of low ranges, most of which are flat-topped, encrusted with laterite. Their slopes are creased with gullies that are filled with great boulders. These are surrounded by immense clumps of spiky grey-green *Triodia* or 'spinifex' grass. And on the slopes, and in the valleys too, grow ghost-gums which are a species of eucalyptus with drooping dark green leaves and smooth sculpted trunks of an exquisite pallor that we cannot really describe in writing.

All in all, this austere country seems to be a pretty good one. Why, then, is it not swarming with animals and people? The trouble, of course, is water or, rather, the lack of it.

That green-grey spinifex and those beautiful ghost-gums exist there comfortably, so to speak, because it was there that they evolved; and they are perfectly adapted to go on living there. There is other vegetation, too, but, in the dry times, little else that moves. Then you will see only the odd wedge-tailed eagle, with a wing-spread of up to ten feet, circling in the distance or, in the dry valley, you will catch a flash of the soft colour of a fleeting euro, a big wallaby, or small kangaroo. The country is beautiful but, seemingly, almost dead.

Rain had fallen just before we passed through and the whole landscape had changed dramatically. Only the brilliant red cliffs remained the same. And because the soil is good, new herbage had sprung up in the valleys. So we saw areas ablaze with the scarlet of Sturt's desert pea and the cerise parakeelia. The whites and yellows and mauves of the hardy 'everlastings' had turned mile after mile into a great wide fairyland.

New animal life had appeared just as suddenly. We saw swarms of finches and parrots and small flocks of orange and crimson chats. 'Chat' is a horrible name for these brilliant robin-sized birds that were already looking after their young. We saw wallabies in small droves, and wheeling overhead were kestrels, harriers and wedge-tailed and whistling eagles. There was an equal abundance of insect life. Blue-tongued stumpy-tailed lizards – 'bobtails' – were plentiful, and in the water-holes, previously parched and covered with hard-caked mud, we saw populations of fairy shrimps and little frogs.

If an ecological niche occurs, life will flow into it, and stay in it, if it is possible that a living can be made. Excluding only the extreme polar regions and the highest, permanently icy sierras the whole dry surface of the earth has been colonized by animals. In many parts of Australia a permanent living cannot be made throughout a year or, sometimes, for several years in succession. In these places, there is a seasonal ebb and flow of life. And the same again. As the seasons change, the living things will come, multiply, and then disperse according to the opportunity the land gives them to reproduce or, even, to stay alive. The same is true of so-called primitive man, for that matter.

Biological success is largely reproductive success. We were travelling through a harshly majestic land that becomes softer and greener and immensely productive only after rain falls. In some parts of the interior this may happen once every few years. Even then the land may remain lush and productive for only two or three months before the sun evaporates the water and withers the new herbage.

The grasses flower and seed quickly after the rains, and the finches and budgerygahs arrive in thousands. One might imagine that George Shaw, the Englishman who first described the budgerygah, must have been familiar not only with its skin, but with the living bird, because he gave it the species name of *undulatus*: the flocks undulate across the sky. Shaw, in fact, never visited Australia and could not have seen them in the air. He may have been told of their great undulating flights, but it seems more likely that the specific name comes from the small wave-like markings on the little parrots' plumage.

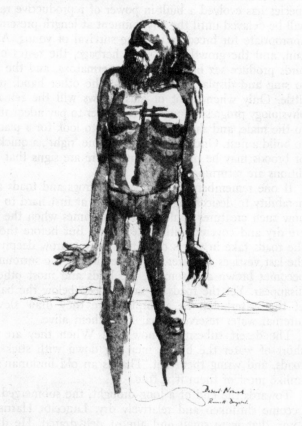

The desert tribesmen are pleasant, gentle people.

In some places almost every hollow eucalyptus branch housed a family of budgerygahs and a single bush sometimes held the bulky nests of thirty finches. When we went by, the doe marsupials were carrying minute young in their pouches. It matters not whether it is spring, summer, or autumn: as long as it is not too cold, the creatures breed after the rains. When the land is green, and the good harvest is there for the taking, the animals 'time' their reproduction and so the young are hatched or dropped at a period when they stand the best chance of survival, and, it follows, the survival of their kind.

One might think that these creatures are supremely intelligent; but of course that is not true. The explanation is that each desert species has evolved a built-in power of reproductive reaction that will be delayed until the environment at length presents a pattern appropriate for breeding and the survival of young. After a little rain, and the growth of a little herbage, the testes of the male birds produce sex hormones and spermatoza, and the birds begin to sing and display. The hens, on the other hand, respond but little. Only when a lot of grass grows will the female internal physiology progress enough to cause her to pay adequate attention to the male, and she will then begin to look for a place in which to build a nest. Once conditions become 'right', a quick succession of broods may be produced until there are signs that desert conditions are returning again.

If one remembers the soft skin of frogs and toads and its vulnerability to desiccating sunshine, it is at first hard to understand how such creatures could survive the times when the water-holes are dry and covered with baked mud. But before the ponds dry the toads take in stores of water. They burrow deeply. Overhead the last vestiges of water evaporate and, as the surrounding valley becomes brown and sombre, the birds and most other creatures disappear. Yet the toads lie safely, deep below the baked surface of the waterholes. In a torpid state they draw slowly on the internal water reservoirs that keep them alive.

The desert tribesmen know this. When they are desperately short of water the brown men dig down with sticks, catch the toads, and wring them out. That is an old bushman's story, but unlike most of them it is true.

Towards the end of a long drought, the submerged toads have become shrunken and relatively dry. Lancelot Harrison dug up some that were small and almost dehydrated. He dropped one into a bucket of water. Within seconds it swelled up and looked like a black knobbly tennis ball. After the rains come, suddenly in the claypans there are full-grown toads, and soon, their young.

The desert tribesmen who dig up and drink water from these water-storing toads are pleasant, gentle people. They are nomads, like the birds and other animals. They live in small communities far from the white man and, by what seems to us an almost super-human hunting ability, manage to keep alive in dry times. The acute development of their sense begins when they are tiny piccaninnies. They can distinguish the individual footprints of every person in the tribe, just as a European knows every face in the village. They can track even tiny lizards across the sun-hardened earth.

One source of their food is the honey-ant. In good times this ant stores honey in its body which then becomes grossly swollen. The nomads discover where the honey-ants make their nests. They dig down with pointed sticks and catch them. Then they squeeze into their mouths the stored honey from the ants' bodies. In good times the desert men, like the other animals, prosper.

L. Mc Clobe   R.J. C

The acute development of their senses begins while they are still piccaninnies.

3

We reached this country by overlanding as did so many of the diggers on the Trail of '86. Like them, and because we were in two parties destined to meet at the Fitzroy Crossing in the Kimberleys on the other side of Australia, we approached from different directions. Marshall and some others set out in two vehicles from Perth, in the south-west, to travel north up and around the continental coastline. The other two, Drysdale and son, began from Sydney, on the eastern coast, to travel inland right across the continent. There our similarity to the miners of seventy-odd years ago ends. Where the pioneers walked, or rode, or drove creaking drays, and warded off the attacks of aborigines, we travelled in carefully equipped motor vehicles. We suffered no hunger, nor were we plagued by thirst. The aborigines that we encountered generally worked as stockmen on the cattle runs, and the odd small family groups we met on their walkabouts were quietly mannered people who smilingly accepted the tobacco and other small comforts that we offered. Over roads that varied from almost immaculate bitumen to corrugated gravel, from hard-baked blacksoil to smothering bulldust, we endured no hardship beyond the fatigue of long hours of driving, or the blatant heat of the inland sun. Bulldust, incidentally, has nothing to do with bulls. It is soft dirt ground to powder.

For those of us who took to the road at Perth there was a northward drive of two thousand miles. For the party that drove from Sydney there was a distance of more than three thousand miles. These are relatively long leads, and in many places there were long dry stretches without surface water or places at which to refuel the vehicles; so we fitted the trucks with long-range fuel and water-tanks.

It was necessary to carry a lot of equipment. Apart from tools and vital spares, there seemed to be a thousand and one articles that we might need. Yet, it is surprising how a load can be reduced when one absolutely must save weight and space. There is hardly anything worse than an over-loaded waggon on a long haul, and the extra work involved in shifting masses of gear (often unnecessary anyway) in order to reach a wanted article, can be a temper wearing process in the heat. On the long wheel-base, station-waggon type of Land Rover we fitted a roof rack. Everyday gear such as tucker-boxes, tools, cameras, dissecting instruments, guns,

The aborigines that we encountered generally worked as stockmen in the cattle runs.

cooking utensils and so on were stored where they could be easily reached. Our rolled swags, which held blankets and a few spare clothes, were stowed in the back. This meant that when we made camp at the end of the day it was a matter of minutes before the proper gear was pulled out and ready for use. After the first few days camping becomes a routine drill. Men quickly remove or return equipment in its accustomed order. Such a routine, too, is good on the nerves of that singularly important character, the camp cook. He is a chap who needs consideration because he has to soldier-on while the others, if they are not out shooting, lounge at ease at the end of the long and dusty days.

If the cook is happy the camp is all right.

From Sydney the best route to the Kimberleys runs inland, north-west to Bourke on the Darling River. From there it crosses the central plains of Queensland to the Leichhardt River, where the big smoke stacks of the Mount Isa silver-lead mines rise incongruously above the ancient hills. Bourke was named after a governor – not the impetuous and incompetent Irish explorer, Burke, who perished. The Leichhardt was named after a gallant but eccentric Prussian whose exact fate is still unknown. This first leg of a thousand miles crosses a landscape that varies from the sandstone escarpments of Sydney harbour and a nearby population of two million people to almost uninhabited open plains. On our first night out we hoped to get as far as possible beyond the Great Divide, the ranges that run like a disarticulated spine right down the eastern coast of Australia. Spring had not yet come and we saw no point in camping in the frosty hills.

The first night's camp always solves a few problems. It brings about rearrangements in the loading that only the practical business of making and breaking camp can do. We knew we would not want to linger in the cold hours of the following daybreak, so that evening we spent a bit of time going over things. This was just as well, for when the first light woke us we found that the canvas coverings over our swags were stiff with frost, and a thin coating of ice rimed the windscreen. We wasted little time in breaking camp and headed for the north, and warmer nights. The road was still bitumen and we could make good time to Nyngan out on the plains. We took advantage of this to ease the new vehicle into a smooth run-in. From Nyngan to Bourke the sky began to open up. The road there runs dead straight and flat for a hundred and thirty miles and, although gravelly and pretty rough in parts, it was good enough for our modest speed.

With thousands of miles ahead of us, it was imperative to keep the vehicles in first-class condition, so we looked after them well, and we had very little trouble.

Sometimes you may be stuck with a broken-down truck a long way out on a lonely track and it can be days before anyone turns up. The only thing to do then is camp. If you are carrying ample water, and enough tucker to keep you going for a couple of weeks, life with a book or two can still be fairly pleasant. But in the scattered pubs of the inland you will hear many stories of the tragedies of people who have perished because they carried insufficient water or (and this has sometimes happened) panicked.

In the bone dry atmosphere of the inland the mid-summer heat sometimes reaches 120 degrees Fahrenheit. This is a scorching, dehydrating temperature, so it is rather important to conserve your body fluids. The quick lizards do this by resorbing the fluid that would be otherwise lost as urine and so they void only a semi-solid mass of crystals. The shy marsupials avoid needless movement in the day's heat; they rest in the deep shadows under the rock faces. Man has no such reptilian device but at least he can think out his problems and copy, if he has sense, the big red 'roo. Exertion will quickly cause exhaustion, and if man cannot replace his sweated fluids he is quickly in a bad way.

Some years ago two men perished from thirst because they tried strenuously to repair their car in the heat of midday. Without water they became hopelessly exhausted, and were eventually found lying dead in the shade of their car. Tragically, they had not been able to think to drain water from the radiator: it was still full, and they were dead alongside. Just two or three days in those conditions and you've had it.

It is interesting, incidentally, that the expression 'had it' originated in the Gulf Country of northern Queensland, where one of us heard it as early as 1929. Oddly enough, the phrase was never current in the populous south before the war. It was taken to Europe by Queensland troops or airmen and there, where lots of chaps were having it, so to speak, it came into general currency. It was circuitously from Europe, and not directly from the north, that the expression reached the southern parts of Australia.

Panic destroys reason. To a stranded man unfamiliar with empty spaces, fear and loneliness can induce a state of anxiety that makes it difficult for him to sit calmly and wait day after day until help comes. There have been men who, well supplied, have been able to stick it out only a couple of days and then, oppressed

17

Station Boss talking with drovers.
R.D. 61.

The station boss always calls the men by their Christian names, and in return the men generally have the same privilege.

by boredom and loneliness, have set out with a water bag in the early morning to walk for help. Such men have sometimes finished the water and then, in desperation, turned back in a vain attempt to reach the security of their truck.

Today, the wireless network spread over the station homesteads prevents many such tragedies. Each homestead is equipped with radio, the only reliable link with the rest of the world. Over the air the station people gossip, call the Flying Doctor if need be, and receive schooling for their children. If you call at these isolated stations they pass ahead word of your coming. If you fail to turn up at the next place they will be out to look for you.

On Australian properties there is an atmosphere of easy informality which extends to the relationship between owner (or manager) and stockmen. The station boss always calls the men by their Christian names and in return the men generally have the same privilege. The owner's wife too calls the men by their first names, but she is usually accorded a formal prefix.

We know of only one woman who ever called men by their surnames. She, a lady of powerful personality and many acres, learned bad habits during visits to Europe. She was much preoccupied with her homestead garden, and she called a succession of gardeners 'Smith', 'Jones', and 'Cholmondeley' as the case would be. After the war, Australian gardeners became highly expensive, and so she recruited a German immigrant called Schitz to do her bidding among the petunias.

She always called this gentleman Rudolph.

We rode over the plains. The nights were warmer now and we lay in our swags, looked up at the vast expanse of the brilliant starlit sky, and watched the sudden drama of a shooting star. The stars here do not twinkle as in Europe: they blaze. And these great plains roll for hundreds of miles in long undulations. Once we pulled up about midday on the road between Tambo and Blackall to boil up for a drink of tea. There was plenty of shade from the coolibahs growing along the banks of a shallow creek that meandered across the plain. It was hot, and the shade was good after the glare of light on the windscreen. Sitting in the dry creek bed we idly noticed that the stream had cut its way through the covering of blacksoil and carved into the hard, compacted underlying sandstone. This rock was crammed with the fossils of tiny marine shells in the sort of abundance that one sees on a sea beach. We were driving over the bed of a long forgotten ocean which has become the pasture land of sheep-farmers.

This is part of what geologists have called the Tambo Sea. It existed about 130 million years ago. There was flooding over much of the earth in those Cretaceous times. The Jurassic bridge between Australia and New Zealand was broken, never to be repaired, 'at least not up till now', as Edgeworth David has said. In the Cretaceous, almost one third of Australia was covered by a great cold, shallow, central sea. This was towards the end of the Mesozoic, or mid-life era. In the remains of this sea have been found the bones of Kronosaurus, a gigantic sea-serpent. This streamlined pliosaur is one of the biggest sea-reptiles yet discovered. It had a great serpentian head, and jaws armed with stabbing blades about ten inches long. Its neck was short, and it sculled its heavy body through the water by means of four powerful paddles. The skull of Kronosaurus was about nine feet long. The wide gape, and massive blade-like teeth, show it to have been a ravenous feeder on large contemporary fishes and reptiles; large mammals had not yet arisen on the earth. Kronosaurus, then, probably behaved in much the same manner as do modern sharks when they snatch, shear and swallow fishes, dolphins and, perchance man, today.

Ice-scratches show on some of the marine rocks in this area. From the outer edges of this great sea-made basin there later seeped down the fresh waters that are imprisoned below – artesian waters that gush up hot and sometimes salty when tapped by bores sunk from the big sheep stations overhead.

Somewhere along here we crossed the track of the disastrous last expedition of Ludwig Leichhardt. In 1848 Leichhardt tried to cross from the Queensland coast to the Swan River settlement – Perth – in Western Australia. Such a job would be difficult even today with all the resources of the internal combustion engine. Leichhardt's expedition disappeared into the desert and apart from the odd tree blazed early on the trip, no authentic traces of it have ever been found. The expedition just vanished. None can tell whether it succumbed to the attacks of aborigines, or whether it was overcome by the pitiless heat of the waterless gibber plains. The tragedy of Leichhardt is complete and mysterious, but some day, somewhere, there must be found relics of the five white men, two aborigines, seven horses, twenty mules, and fifty bullocks that went into the wilderness never to return.

The road beyond Winton, a typical western town set in a landscape of golden grass, runs flat like a board for miles. Occasional stunted trees marked the courses of small streams that were dry when we passed through. The sky pressed down on the land, and the horizon moved to meet it in a shimmering haze. The hard-beaten surface of the blacksoil seemed to stretch on forever. In the hot dry weather this covering of blacksoil compacts into a solid, cement-like surface over which one can travel fast. Yet a mere thirty points of rain will turn it to glutinous bog in which vehicles get hopelessly stuck. To be bogged in the blacksoil is not very funny, and the breezes that float over the plains could be loaded with echoes of the language of men that have cursed them. We were reminded of the blacksoil of another place and of that stalwart of Australian folklore, the dog that sat on the tucker-box.

> As I was coming down Conroy's Gap
> I heard a maiden cry,
> 'There goes Bill the bullocky,
> He's bound for Gundagai.
> A better poor old bastard

> Never earnt an honest crust,
> A better poor old bastard
> Never drug a whip through dust.'
> His team got bogged at the Five Mile Creek,
> Bill lashed and swore and cried,
> 'If Nobby don't get me out of this,
> I'll tattoo his bloody hide.'
> But Nobby strained and broke the yoke,
> And poked out the leader's eye,
> Then the dog sat on the tucker-box
> Five miles from Gundagai.

And the latter-day Word, according to Jack Moses:

> I've been jilted, jarred and crossed in love
> And sandbagged in the dark,
> Till, if a mountain fell on me,
> I'd treat it as a lark.
> It's when you've got your bullocks bogged
> That's the time you flog and cry,
> And the dog sits on the tucker-box
> Nine miles from Gundagai.[1]

The lumbering bullock waggons of earlier days, packed high with bales of wool and moving like broad-beamed barges across the plains, were often bogged to the axles in the sticky black ooze. No wonder that the bullockys possessed a vocabulary unsurpassed in its invective and fluency. The truckers of today let fly in the same tradition, for spinning wheels in blacksoil mud can produce a sense of frustration beyond almost anything in creation. There still exist people who proclaim that the damnation of man is encompassed with brimstone and fire, but there are many gentlemen in the west who would settle smartly for brimstone if offered it as a choice from blacksoil mud.

Before we got to the little township of McKinlay, acacia and eucalyptus scrub appeared. Then, as we approached Cloncurry, the plains gave way to rocky broken hills. In these formations have been found rich deposits of uranium. Here the soil is poor and lightly grassed, and the hills have an old and battered look. Cloncurry, generally called 'The Curry', is the western Queensland

[1] The penultimate line in each jingle is sometimes varied to suit a particular audience.

A hundred and twenty miles past The Isa we reached Camooweal.

base of the incomparable Flying Doctor Service (which for some inscrutable reason recently had wished on it the prefix 'Royal') whose operations extend in a great arc for hundreds of miles.

Thirty or forty miles beyond The Curry is the new uranium field and mining town of Mary Kathleen. A modern township, with lawns, shade trees and a broad bitumen road running in from Cloncurry, Mary Kathleen makes a startling contrast to the usual rambling western town. We were pleased to hit that road after the long dusty run from Winton. The last thirty miles before Mount Isa brought us back to reality. Here was one of the worst stretches of the lot. Rough, and full of rocky outcrops, the road winds up and down into stony-bottomed gullies and over broken ridges. It was not until we got within a few miles of The Isa that we could call it a road again. At The Isa we serviced the vehicles and bought stores before starting a four-hundred mile run west along excellent bitumen over the Barkly Highway. This, and the Stuart Highway, the thousand-mile road that runs north from Alice Springs to Darwin, were built to carry military traffic during the Japanese War.

A hundred and twenty miles past The Isa we reached Camooweal. We pulled up at the verandah of the long wooden pub late

A quiet buzz advertised a session within.

on a Sunday afternoon. The bar doors were closed in proper deference to the Sabbath but a quiet buzz advertised a session within. We walked round the back of the pub and then into the bar where a dozen station hands and drovers were yarning and drinking cold beer. Soon we were asking and answering the usual questions about the road, the season, our destination and those of the men lounging around. One of the blokes looked vaguely familiar. We had met him two years before.

Inevitably he alluded to that meeting as having taken place 'the other day'. Everything out here took place the other day. This casual indifference to time has great charm, but it is apt to be somewhat disturbing if you accept it literally. There are plenty of strangers who have waited hopefully for a lift for weeks from some gentleman who promised to turn up in 'a day or two'. They always *do* turn up; but on occasions their elastic evaluation of the time can be disconcerting.

We left Camooweal and crossed the dry bed of the Georgina River. Through the coolibah trees we saw again the flat plain extending ahead. In the two years that had gone since we saw it last an odd change had occurred. Where the plain in the immediate vicinity of Camooweal was formerly littered only with the brown glass of innumerable discarded beer bottles, it now glistened in the evening sun with what we took to be thousands of white gibbers. These were empty beer cans. In the last two years canned beer – good Melbourne beer – had become extremely popular. It chills quickly. Tins are lighter, more readily packed and do not easily break. The can itself can act as a mug. Hence the new look in the landscape.

A few miles on from Camooweal we reached the fence bordering the Northern Territory. Beside the road stands a large metal strip, a little pompously, it seemed to us, telling the traveller, as though he didn't know, that he is now about to enter the Commonwealth Territory of the Northern Territory. It was pleasant to find this silly notice to be barely decipherable. The light-hearted citizens of the Barkly Tableland had riddled it with bullets.

The next township would be Tennant Creek, another 300 miles on. Between these settlements the road crosses a vast, almost

One of the blokes. R.D. 61

One of the blokes looked vaguely familiar. We had met him two years before.

treeless, plain. The few trees that exist generally grow along shallow meandering watercourses that flow only in the summer 'wet'. They then shrink to isolated water-holes and lagoons in the dry months of winter. Driving across these plains is rather like being at sea in a small boat. We were, in fact, travelling over the former bed of yet another great shallow inland sea. This sea, however, existed about 400 million years earlier than the one whose animals we saw in the creek at Tambo. It rippled in Cambrian times, and in the coral-like (but not true coral) limestones beneath the black-soil, geologists have found horizon after horizon of marine fossils, many exquisitely preserved after 500 million years of burial. This great sea, sprawling north and south right across the continent from the Kimberleys to Adelaide, once split Australia into two huge islands.

The blacksoil, spread thinly above this ancient seabed, ran flat to the horizon as far as we could see. The blacksoil is covered with a rich growth of Mitchell grass, named, like the pink- and yellow-crested Major Mitchell cockatoo, after an early explorer. The porosity of the underlying limestone has allowed the accumulation of artesian reservoirs. When these are tapped by bores the water spurts upwards on to the plain. Here are the biggest cattle stations (*not* ranches) in the world.

Alexandria Downs, for example, covers about 11,262 square miles. You have to go about one hundred miles from the front gate to get to the homestead. It is not true that you can put the whole of the state of Texas in this single rather large property, but it is a fact that Alexandria Downs is about the size of Belgium. The station maintains its own small hospital, for the nearest public medical centre is the Cloncurry base of the flying doctor about 350 miles away. Alexandria Downs runs 70,000 head of cattle. The horse paddock covers 10,000 acres and there are 1,500 horses. It takes twenty-five whites and about a hundred aborigines to run the place, and fifty-six bores give it water. Victoria Downs was once even bigger, but this station was cut up about twelve years ago, and so Alexandria will hold pride of place until it, too, is sub-divided for closer settlement.

The store cattle bred on the Barklys are driven on the hoof south-east to the fattening areas of Queensland. It is a good sight in the winter months of the dry season to see the great mobs drifting over the plains in the charge of a droving team. The stock-men (*not* cowboys) spend months in the saddle, for they ride the mob constantly. A drover's outfit consists of the boss drover and

The drovers bring the mob to water each afternoon.

half a dozen or more hands, a cook, a plant of thirty or forty horses and sometimes mules and, nowadays, a three-ton truck to carry gear and tucker. The truck usually goes ahead each day to the next bore. These bores are spaced about twenty miles apart along the stock routes, and so the drovers find their next camp already made when they bring the mob to water each afternoon.

Today, most of the droving outfits are made up of half-caste and full-blood aboriginal stockmen. These men excel at the game. They are magnificent horsemen; an astonishing thing because, until Burke and Wills came through in 1860, the only domestic animal this country had ever seen was the dingo dog. Yet to look at these aboriginal stockmen you would think they were born to the saddle. They have about them such an air of easy, relaxed grace.

The road is excellent and we made good time. Yet it was monotonous and tiring, driving due west into the afternoon sun which came glaring up off the bitumen. We were glad to pull into the small combined pub and store at Frewena for a drink and a spell. This is the only spot where you can get petrol on the lead of 300 miles between Camooweal and Tennant Creek. We, in fact, had plenty of fuel in our long-range tanks but we were glad of the break under the cool verandah. We reached Tennant Creek in the evening and bought ourselves the national dish of steak and eggs at a cafe before heading north to find a camp. Then came an uneventful run north on the Stuart Highway to the pleasant little town of Katherine. We were glad to be there, because now we could start on the last thousand miles to the Fitzroy over on the western coast of the continent. From The Katherine onwards we could expect the worst roads. The Dry River

26

track is notorious for bulldust and for the broken limestone outcrops out west near Wave Hill.

One hundred and eighty miles on we reached Top Springs, a lonely watering place at the head of the Murranji stock route. This track carries the mobs of cattle that are driven east to the Barklys and then on down to Queensland. There is a small store at The Springs and here the droving outfits restock, and replenish gear. The present season was very dry, and there was no surface water on the Dry River road. We refilled our tanks and recalled an experience on this track two years before when we picked up a curious gentleman about twenty miles out on the plain. He had set out on foot to walk from The Katherine to Top Springs, carrying only a blanket, a billy-can, one tin of meat and half a

Young Stockman
Reserves Droving

The stockmen (not cowboys) *spend months in the saddle, for they ride the mob constantly.*

gallon of water. There is not much traffic on this road. His meagre supply of water could not have lasted him long. When we met him he was clad only in shirt, trousers and a pair of broken sand-shoes. He had no hat. He rode with us to The Springs, offering no explanation for his crazy walk. One gets used to oddities in the inland.

This time the road was worse than before. There had been no grader over it since the winter, and the rains of the previous 'wet' had cut it up badly. The mud of the 'wet' had been powdered into fine bulldust of the consistency of talcum powder. In some places the bulldust lay almost a foot deep. It was dangerous if hit by a vehicle at speed, for steering is then almost impossible and so it is easy to lose control and sideswipe a tree. After a few miles in this dust we found it penetrating everywhere. It rose in clouds, and we could feel and hear it *whoosh* against the floorboards each time we struck a crook patch. In the intense heat the sweat trickled down our chests and made mud. The gritty taste of dust was always in our mouths.

We were often thirsty and were glad that the water bags were slung readily accessible in front of the vehicle. Here the constant evaporation from the bags kept the water deliciously cool just as the evaporation of sweat keeps a man cool in a dry, but not humid, climate. We could not travel fast along the track winding in and out of the scrub. It took us a good day's drive to cover the 180 miles to Top Springs. We crossed a timbered creek where some aborigines were camped, climbed the opposite bank to the store and pulled the vehicle to a stop.

A remarkable store this, set in the middle of nowhere. It carries an extraordinary variety of goods: hardware, saddlery, clothes, firearms and food; all the necessities that the traveller is likely to want, and a good many other things as well. Since we were through before, the storekeeper had got a liquor licence. This was a sound move. He handed us some cold cans of lager. After the dust and sweat of that particular drive these were wonderful. Then we found that the bumpy road had loosened a couple of rivet heads in the long-range petrol tank. This let the tank weep, so we had to get some four gallon tins and transfer the petrol to them until we might reach some place where we could re-solder the rivets. These rivets held in place the baffle plates which divided the interior of the tank. The baffles were designed to stop the excessive movement of petrol as we drove over rough country, but the manufacturers had spaced the rivets too far apart. The result was that too much strain of the slopping liquid was imparted to too few rivets, causing the slight fractures.

Neither were the twin water bag carriers bolted to the front fender satisfactory under the conditions. They allowed the canvas bags to swing and fray against the stanchions. One bag was now holed, and the other was wearing and rapidly going the same way. We solved this problem by buying a broom, sawing off the handle and lashing it across the front of the vehicle. To the broom handle we strapped new bags so that they could now swing free without rubbing against metal.

The sun was setting when we left Top Springs. It was a dull red ball in a sky laden with dust and gave the bush a ruddy glow, the sort of evening glow that appears after a day of bushfires when the warm air is filled with rising smoke. But the next day dawned bright and clear with a cool early morning wind. We were now free of the bulldust, for the track became stony and the first outcrops of limestone began to appear. Great slabs of it had been weathered out of the earth, compelling us to crawl in low gear in the manner of a military tank rolling over obstacles. In other parts, sharp shales that had been upended in former geological times kept progress slow. The early morning is good to drive in for the air is fresh and without heat; and the light is clear gold and sparkling. Also, the wild life is out using the few hours before the sun climbs high and the heat descends on the land.

We saw the big red 'roos pause and prop. In turn, they watched us curiously and with caution as we passed. Running through a clump of trees we would come suddenly on pairs of plain turkeys, properly bustards, that would break into an awkward trot and then with heavily flapping wings, take to the sky.

The Australian bustard has become a rare sight on the plains and in the sparse open forests of the inland. It has a wing-span of up to seven feet and may weigh as much as 32 lbs. Prettily, though sombrely, marked in brown and fawn, black and white, it was one of the first land birds remarked upon in Australia. Not, however, for its beauty, nor for its slightly cumbrous charm, but for the quality of its flesh which, though perhaps a little 'dry', is welcome to hungry men. The English navigator Cook, first to sail along the eastern coast of Australia, named a bay after it in thanksgiving in May 1770. 'At dinner we ate the bustard. It turned out an excellent bird, far the best; we all agreed, that we had eaten since we left England; and as it weighed fifteen pounds, our dinner was not only good but plentiful.'

A close relative of this bird was once common on the downs of England but there they were mercilessly exterminated. When the early British arrived in Australia they ran true to form and massacred almost everything in sight for meat, fur, or sport. In recent years there has developed in Australia a sharp revulsion against the former slaughter. Nowadays, you are apt to see displayed in bush post-offices colourful notices urging the preservation of the bustard.

Today, even in the suburbs of the capital cities, possums scamper about the leafy streets. Sometimes one is startled to see an echidna, an egg-laying 'living fossil' related to the platypus, appear mysteriously in a suburban park. Nor is the local fauna nowadays ravaged by that pest, the egg collector, whose noisome activities in Britain necessitate the posting of a protective guard on the nests of certain rare birds on the occasions they build there. In Australia the pendulum has swung so emphatically towards protection that in some states *bona fide* scientists have been refused permits to take specimens of relatively common animals.

Nevertheless, two considerable dangers still remain.[1] First, many southern European migrants kill and eat any small bird whenever they can; and secondly, rural politicians, obedient to local pressures, often oppose the establishment of new faunal reserves and sometimes try to alienate those already established. Attempts to protect individuals of a species are useless if the habitat in which they evolved is destroyed. Usually this has been done to make room for another few thousand acres of wheat or some more bananas. A near criminal act of such alienation was perpetrated some years ago in Tasmania when a section of a national park full of mountain ash, some of which were three hundred feet high and as big as the Californian redwoods, was thrown open to a commercial concern for the manufacture of paper pulp.

Crossing the plains we were always aware of a brilliant variety of parrots that flashed in the sunlight. At the windmill and tank of almost every bore we disturbed flocks of galahs. Those grey and rose-pink cockatoos swirled into the sky, seemingly in thousands, the early sunlight turning their breast feathers to a rich and glowing madder. Their tumultuous screeching rent the air. This was an exhilarating sight. Occasionally we saw emus

[1] This was written before there arose the establishment of the iniquitous trade in kangaroo meat.

stalking warily amongst the trees or out on the open plain. These flightless birds, the next largest after the ostrich, are of an inquisitive disposition. If you stop the truck they will often turn about and advance hesitantly. A spanner or stone knocked against metal will sometimes bring them forwards. But when alarmed they gallop off at wild speed, sometimes with a number of striped chickens pounding at their heels.

About twenty miles from Wave Hill cattle station we came across a young fellow whose big semi-trailer had broken down. The generator had packed up and his starting handle had broken. He was camped under the trailer. Here he had lain contentedly for the past two days. He had any amount of petrol, he said, as well as a forty-four-gallon drum of water and plenty of tucker. He was supremely unconcerned, explaining that 'in a day or two' his mate would be along with another truck and then they would be able to carry out repairs. He had been carrying a load of building materials from Darwin to Hooker Creek, seventy or eighty miles south of Wave Hill. Hooker Creek is an outpost station of the Native Welfare Department and is situated in an aboriginal reservation on the northern fringe of the desert. The driver lay in his swag away from the sun. He fed spinifex pigeons and finished two books. He told us he had soon made friends with these pretty little birds when they came to investigate him.

We hauled some soldering kit out of our vehicle, but after a few attempts to fix the generator we had to give the game away. The sun was brazen overhead and the stony ground reflected the heat. We boiled up a billy and opened some canned meat and suggested that we might let Wave Hill know of his breakdown. Then, while stowing away the soldering kit, we suddenly remembered that our starting handle was a very long one. We pulled it out and found that it fitted the heavy truck. Two or three turns and the big motor turned over sweetly. The young fellow rolled his swag and heaved his gear aboard. He said that he could keep her running in the flat country to Hooker Creek.

We waved goodbye and started off along the track. Before reaching Wave Hill we turned right and made for the crossing over the Victoria River. Here the country breaks into low hills, pale gold in the sun. Just beyond the Victoria is Wave Hill police station. This lonely outpost is manned by a single constable, his wife and some 'black' trackers. After a drink of tea and a yarn we set off in the direction of the Western Australian border, now only a hundred and ninety miles away. The trooper told us that, apart from a bad patch of limestone not far ahead, the road was pretty good all the way to Hall's Creek. We pushed on into scrub country where the going was slowed up by the limestone. Here the country was extremely dry, for they had had a poor 'wet' previously.

As the sun slid down near the horizon we camped. The moon was nearly full and the bush was beautiful and mysterious in the soft light. It was still and quiet except for the puttering of the fire. Somehow one could sense the feeling of the vast space outside. The bush is enchanting by night, but it can be lonely too. Around the campfire we read some old Sydney newspapers that a traveller from Darwin had given us at The Katherine and which we had forgotten were in the truck. We seemed so unutterably remote from traffic problems, politics, universities and night clubs that the accounts of city life read like stories of another world. We studied the social pages with relish. It was pleasant to read of Mrs Pauncefote at barbecue beside the harbour. We dined by our fire on corned beef helped along by pannikins of black, sweet tea. Then we lay back in our swags and watched the moon ride high. We were extremely happy. There is a singular sense of relaxation when you are camped down comfortably many hundreds of miles from the centres of civilization. You come to understand that your real needs are simple indeed.

As usual we broke camp early. For the rest of the run to Hall's Creek we were on good roads. It was good to think that we would meet the southern party soon and we wondered just where they might be. Then we crossed the Western Australian border, and ran over the plain towards the bore just outside Nicholson Station. It was pretty bare of feed here and cattle were bunched about the water troughs. Carcases reflected the state of the country and so did the crows and kites that flapped away at our approach. Soon we were looking at the distant ranges of the southern Kimberleys.

Now the road began to run among the bare and rocky hills that had lured the miners to the Hall's Creek rush on the Trail of '86. We knew that we were not late for our rendezvous at the Fitzroy Crossing, and so we reckoned that we could afford time to put up for the night at Rob Moody's pub where, additionally, we could repair the long-range petrol tank. As we approached the town we saw feral donkeys clambering up the rocky slopes. These are the descendants of animals that escaped, or were sometimes liberated, from the early mining camps. They are now pests in

Rob Moody not only builds a pub, but an atmosphere at the same time.

parts of the Kimberleys; they roam the plains of the Fitzroy in thousands and compete seriously for grass so that the cattlemen organize shoots to reduce their numbers.

And so we came to the Old Town at Hall's Creek, a handful of battered remnants of the gold miners' dreams. Today the gold has gone, but the dreams remain, for odd old prospectors still fossick in the hills in search of shotty gold.

Rob Moody is building a new pub. He is building it in the New Town. This lies on the flat ground where you can land a 'plane – about ten miles from the old place. Moody is putting the pub up in a desultory fashion; nobody ever hurried Moody. He not only builds a pub, but an atmosphere at the same time.

At the age of eighteen Moody accompanied Canning when he surveyed the Canning Stock Route, one of the most pitiless cattle trails in the west. It leads 1,000 miles from Hall's Creek to Wiluna, across swelling fixed sand dunes, desert and mulga. Those days, in 1906, wild brown stone-age people roamed this country which was their own. In a sparse uncharitable land they dared not leave the water-holes and soaks in times of drought. When the country was bare they accepted the slightest manna from heaven. For example, when pigeons fly daily out of the desert to the water-holes to drink they are replete with the fruits of distant shrubs which the aborigines themselves could not reach. The birds are nourished by the fleshy part of the fruit, and they void the

33

stones at the drinking places. These the natives sifted and washed. Then they ground the stones on the flat river rocks and used the paste to eke out their bare living in times of hunger.

Moody remains as a link between us and these fat-smeared suspicious men, remnants of whom still exist, farther inland still, secret and hidden from the sight of an alien civilization. Most of Moody's life has been spent in wild places. One of the other party had known him in New Guinea before the war. Later Moody talked of the men they had known around Aitape and Wewak, most of whom had since been killed by Melanesian spears or, a bit later, in the Japanese War. Now Moody was back beyond the Kimberleys where he had started his wanderings more than fifty years ago – active, philosophical and humorous in a sort of argumentative eventide.

'They think they're tough out here,' he said, 'but you can beat 'em away with your hat.

'Y'know, they always make the same mistake. They try to climb over the bar to hit you. And, you know, when they've got their hands and feet full of bar you can king-hit them with no trouble at all.'

Moody beamed pleasantly in retrospect.

'Of course, some of them pick themselves up out of a corner and come twice. But I've never known one to come back a third time.'

We resoldered the long-range tank and started off on the last lap towards the western coast of Australia and our rendezvous with the southern party at Fitzroy Crossing.

The road was a very different proposition from two years ago. Then it was mostly a rough track; now it was a graded road. We passed the dreaming mountains of the Emmanuel Range that stand stark and flat-topped against the sky. On the bare plain before them, as though marching in ranks into the distance, were thousands of anthills. They gave the impression of some strange and vast cemetery whose gaunt, eroded headstones were all that was left of another race.

Yet beneath each of these seemingly simple mounds of clay was a teeming city of chambers and inter-linking thoroughfares built by millions of wood-eating insects. They digest the wood by the aid of a population of simple organisms that live in their intestines. If you kill off this symbiotic gut population with X-rays, without injuring the host, the termite will die of indigestion for it cannot by its own means digest wood any more than we can.

As well as trees – including live ones – termites tend to devour telegraph poles, fences, railway sleepers and houses. This results in an inestimable amount of damage in tropical Australia. Generally they are called 'white ants', but they are rarely really white, and they bear no anatomical resemblance to any ant. Termites, in fact, occupy a zoological order by themselves.

The mounds here were relatively small, a mere six feet high. In the Gulf Country these minute insects erect castles, riddled with millions of dark passages and chambers, to a height of twenty feet. Here, too, live the magnetic termites which raise relatively thin slab-like 'tomb-stones', all pointing north and south, with their broad sides facing in a way that allows them to get the maximum drying and warming effects of the sun.

Like true ants and bees, termites have an elaborate caste system. Both workers and soldiers are sterile. The workers are usually blind and wingless, and have big heads and heavy jaws with which they chew their woody food. They build and repair, stock the nest with food, tend the special fungus gardens, carry out sanitation duties, feed and groom the queen, and look after her eggs and young. The soldiers, too, are wingless, and in most species blind. The soldier's head is equipped with a powerful horny armoury and, in many species, sharp jaws and a special forehead gland that produces an irritant that can be discharged against

On the bare plains, as though marching in ranks into the distance, were thousands of anthills.

invaders. These defend their queen, the colony, and provide guards for parties of foraging workers. There seems to be good evidence that, in some species at least, soldiers sound the alarm by beating the gallery walls with their armoured heads.

The males and females have wings, and relatively good eyesight. At intervals the workers chisel holes in the walls of the mound, and the males and females then swarm out of the old termitarium and fly short distances to found new colonies. As they leave the nest, the native tribesmen gather and eat them. Once, in Uganda, one of us was offered a species that had a pleasant, somewhat nutty flavour, although, as invertebrate food goes, he would have preferred oysters or *Homard à la Newburg*.

Soon after leaving the nest the sexual termites shake off their wings. A pair will dig a hole, the beginning of a new nest and colony. A pregnant female will swell into a queen that, once the splinter colony is established, spends the rest of her life in what becomes the royal cell, laying several thousand eggs a day in the new establishment. Meanwhile the clay mound is made bigger, and its subterranean tunnels are driven in all directions towards stumps, logs, houses and other objects that provide food. Some species cultivate gardens of fungi that supply additional food. This complicated organization would seem to indicate a conscious intelligence but of course there is none. Termites and other insects have no true brain in their nervous system. Their activities, however remarkable in their evolution and final organization, are purely reflex and mechanical.

We saw thousand upon thousand of these conical colonies on our way to the flood plain of the Fitzroy River. Here tall river gums grew thickly. We crossed on a low-level concrete causeway that had been newly built across the wide sandy bed. There was no flow, but isolated pools of water lay here and there up and down stream. Beneath the sands there lies a great reservoir of water that is tapped by bores to supply the little settlement. Along the northern bank is a little hospital serviced by a Flying Doctor. There is a post office, a police station and the pub. The pub is also a large store. Each of these buildings is widely separated from its neighbour so that there is no township in the formal sense. Nor are there any streets. The wooden buildings stand among tall shady eucalypts. They are built on piles so that the river cannot flood into them during the 'wet'. This also helps to defeat termites.

Dick Fallon and his wife run the pub and store. Dick is a big and friendly man who has spent many years in the Kimberleys.

He is one of those pleasant-tempered men who lets nothing bother him. Sometimes he finds it necessary to be firm with the occasional obstreperous character. He will go out of his way to help, or advise when asked, and is possessed of that engaging quality that does not demand explanation or reasons, but accepts the fact that a man ought to know best what he wants and why he wants it. If you have not seen Dick for years, he will calmly carry on from where you left off. There is about him an air of self-sufficiency and permanence, so that it is difficult to think of The Crossing without him. Dick had just built a bigger store, and was finishing a new bar with three sides open to help keep the citizens cool. This pub has been on The Crossing since the early days of the Kimberleys, and has the character and charm of an old establishment. The Fallons could give us no word of the southern party. So, on the next day, we set out to meet them. We knew that their progress would be slower than ours since they had to visit some off-shore islands and would be collecting zoological specimens all the way.

From the Fitzroy Crossing it is a two hundred mile run to the coastal town of Derby (pronounced as spelt) on a pretty good road. We headed coastwards, thinking we might pick them up along the track. We had no luck. At Derby we saw the Indian Ocean. We had crossed the continent from the Pacific. We drank a lot of cold beer and then went to the post office and rang the Fisheries Inspector at Broome about 130 miles south. We reckoned that he would know if there was a team of zoologists in the area. He did, too. He said that the other party had left town early on the previous evening and that they could reach Fitzroy Crossing next day. We realized now that we had probably let them pass while we were in Derby. So now we back-tracked hurriedly along the road to the Fitzroy Crossing.

We caught their trail from a couple of road workers who had seen a convoy pass an hour before. One said: 'I'll draw yer a mud map the way they went.'

In the late afternoon we rounded a bend in the pindan scrub and reached West Hardman Creek. On the opposite bank were their vehicles, pulled off the road for the evening camp. We pulled in, too, and were greeted by Dominic Serventy and Ivan Carnaby. The other one was in the nearby timber shooting specimens. He very soon appeared. It was a good meeting. The southern party had come two thousand miles. The eastern party had come three thousand. We had met within a day and forty miles according

Working for the Man
Reader's Board
Donald Somebody...

'I'll draw yer a mud map the way they went.'

to arrangements made weeks before over some grog up at The Cross in Sydney. There was much talk of what had happened to each other on our respective journeys. We were well pleased. Then there was a rush for pannikins. Dom had let the moths out of his pocket in Broome, and was flourishing a bottle of Scotch.

4

In sharp contrast, the other party had rarely been far from the ocean, and often on it. It would be logical at the present moment to begin the story of their journey up the coast from Perth to our meeting at the West Hardman and this we would do were it not for one grave and important question: Do Europeans believe that modern Australia is composed essentially of kangaroos and stringybarks?

We may be performing an inestimable service to better Commonwealth understanding if we interleave with our story the following lines. You would not have the benefit of this vital information had one of us not shared a very agreeable reunion with an old friend in London after our return there.

This friend is G. S. Watson, Chief Migration Officer at Australia House in the Strand. After the publication by the London *Observer* of a series of articles out of which the more or less sensible part of this book is growing, we had a few noggins together in The Surrey. Once we had been brother company commanders. We had not met since.

'I suppose I enjoyed your articles,' said Andy Watson, 'but they won't help potential migrants to decide to go to Australia.'

A Briton, if approved at Australia House, can get to Australia for £10. Most Australians in Britain, which generally means London, gain some small understanding of the Englishman's liking for his green sponge, his right little tight little isle, but usually they are genuinely astounded that he should not, if given the opportunity, lay back his ears and rush for the nearest boat into more comfortable living, higher wages, the cool green surf and the sunshine.

Although we do not belong to this school, Mr Watson's professional judgement on the articles, justly acclaimed in other circles to be superb, was disturbing.

'What do you mean?'

'Well,' he said, 'you stressed the usual dismal themes – space, gum trees, red dust, heat, beer and kangaroos. Thank God you didn't mention cricket; that would have been the bloody end.'

'There's nothing dismal about a pint of Cascade,' we said. 'Anyway, what did you expect us to write about? – the Sydney Symphony, the poetry of Judith Wright, the painting of William Dobell, the virus research of Sir Macfarlane Burnet or the new elevated expressway that flies off the Harbour Bridge over Circular Quay?'

'You might well have mentioned them,' said Mr Watson calmly. 'Also, it would have been a good idea if you had given a line or so to the exciting domestic architecture, the great steel and glass office buildings, the standards of living enjoyed by Australians compared with those of these people here; the excellent restaurants and the superb domestic air services, the trains that tend to run on time and the extraordinary proportion of books sold per head of population; the concert artists like Joan Sutherland, Joan Hammond and Eileen Joyce, and, oddly enough, that the average Australian child has a rather greater likelihood of singing at La Scala or Covent Garden, or being represented at the New York Museum of Modern Art, than has the child in England.'

Mr Watson was merely warming up.

'You could have mentioned too, that, in Australia, typists save up and buy original oils. You could have noticed the Australian research on rain-making, ecology, trace elements in animal nutrition, and radio-physics. The great new Opera House rising on the shores of Sydney Harbour, and the new Arts Centre, with gallery, theatre, underground car parks and the like, that they've started in Melbourne. The new universities springing up. The Mediterranean atmosphere of Kings Cross, Sydney. After all, these matters are

40

more typical of modern Australia than Harmonious Jack, Whispering Bill, Brandy Smith and your slightly sordid little outback pubs.'

'You,' Andy concluded, 'are writing nostalgically about the Australia of Banjo Paterson, Henry Lawson and the bush balladists of the nineties.'

5

Back to the wallabies and paperbarks. As we said, the southern party had rarely been far from the ocean. At first they numbered three – Dr Dominic Serventy, of the Commonwealth Scientific and Industrial Research Organization, Ken Buller, a taxidermist from the Western Australian Museum and Marshall. We left Perth in a spring dawn. We rode in Dom Serventy's Land Rover, which hauled a trailer, inland and north-west of the small town of Yalgoo. There had been good rain here, and the whole of south-western Australia seemed to be carpeted with flowers. There were acres and acres of them – and then more acres. They were yellow, mauve, white and pink: whole slopes of colour, with orange and scarlet chats, pink galahs, red-tailed black cockatoos and charming little native hens vieing with the flowers in colourful display. The flowers would soon fade, but while at their best they were sheer glory.

We took on petrol at the parched western town of Morawa just after lunch-time on the first day out. Here the hard-baked earth is covered by an even harder capstone. In the heat of high summer, so the local story runs, it is necessary to start digging a grave soon after it seems that it will be required. Otherwise, it might not be quite ready when it is, in fact, needed. It is tough work digging in such country, and so they hit on the idea of quickly blasting a hole in the cemetery by means of gelignite whenever somebody had to have one. But the cemetery at Morawa was near the hospital and the matron asked the grave diggers to revert to more conventional implements. She said that at the sound of blasting other patients tended to 'take a turn for the worse'.

During our lunch stops, and at the evening camp, it was pleasant to hear the tinkle of bellbirds in the mulga. The melody of the bellbird was heard and described years before the collection of the hidden singer. Quoy, a French surgeon-naturalist in de Freycinet's *Uranie*, was in Sharks Bay in 1818 and he heard the bellbird on one of his collecting trips ashore. 'A very strange bird is the one whose call resembles the sound of a little bell that is struck abruptly. It is heard only at sunrise and we were pleased to listen to it, though without being able to distinguish its author.'

It was not until a decade later that the author of the little bell itself found its way into scientific literature. One can understand how a green European might fail to collect this elusive brown, black-crested ventriloquist. It is not easy to see either when calling up in a mulga, or foraging on the leaf-strewn floor of the scrub. The aborigines' onomatopoeic name *pan-pan-panella* prettily does justice to the ventriloquial two slow notes and the three that closely follow.

At Yalgoo, Ivan Carnaby, a naturalist and kangaroo shooter of local celebrity, added himself and his battered blue Dodge utility truck to the party. Ivan was a welcome addition. He has considerable knowledge of the local fauna. It was Ivan who located a small flock of native hens beside a swampy stream between Yalgoo and Geraldton. We were delighted to see these peculiarly attractive little fowl about which some of us had heard so much, but had never seen. They go in small flocks. They are about as big as a bantam and are feathered dark bronze-brown, a colour relieved by a horny forehead shield of pea-green and legs of brick-red. Thannimidi, the East Murchison aborigines called them. In 1833, a tribe near Perth surprisingly described them as 'the white men's birds'.

The veteran collector John Gilbert, who was later speared to death on Cape York, gave this information. He, and John Hutt, an early Governor of the Swan River settlement, were astonished by a phenomenon that has since become well known – the sudden irruption of thousands of pretty little hens into places that have not seen them within living memory. Gilbert said that the birds 'treaded' down whole fields of corn in a single night; the situation must have resembled that of the memorable ball of Kirrimuir. The local aborigines, not having seen the little hens before, attributed their visit to the newly arrived whites; hence, 'white men's birds'. However, it's an ill wind, and all that, for it is recorded also that thousands of them were shot and eaten by the meat-hungry settlers. Other irruptions from nowhere, so to speak, came in 1853, 1886 and 1897 and there have been several during the present century. Once the small hens made free with parks and gardens in the heart of the state capital.

On the way back towards the coast at Geraldton we ran close beside a railway line. We saw no trains, but they still run occasionally. Dom said that some such railways have fallen completely into disuse because they are unable to compete with the heavy trucks that nowadays bring wool and other produce more cheaply and quickly in from the back country. It is always a little sad to see rusting rails, and we were reminded of another railway we once knew in north Queensland, away over on the other side of the continent. That was one built during a gold rush in the closing years of the last century. It was designed to open up a large area of country but after eighty miles of construction, the gold field petered out and the railway almost did too. When we were last there there was but one train a week to take supplies up-country to a small pub, a police station and a post-office. This railway bears no resemblance to any normal once except that it consists of rails and sleepers, and over it runs what the State Railways Department optimistically calls rolling stock. The prime mover is a diesel rail motor which for all the world resembles one of those charabancs that plied the English countryside in the 1920's. Open to the air, and hooded, it carries slings for the accommodation of rifles and water bags. Emmett himself could not have dreamed up a more Emmett-like creature.

The driver, Bill, held this office as one of many duties. He was also stationmaster, conductor, porter and ticket-collector. To ride with Bill on the front seat was an exhilarating experience. He leant nonchalantly back in his seat, hat over eyes to shade them from the glare. With the toe of one bare foot hooked around the dashboard accelerator Bill would point out places of no special interest.

As we looked ahead we saw little sign of the rails because the kangaroo grass grew three or four feet high. This gave the impression of driving a reaping machine through a field of red wheat at forty miles an hour. While jouncing from side to side in this machine, which he informed us was known as Leaping Lena or the Abortion Express, Bill espied a figure in the grass ahead. Squinting through the cracked windscreen Bill said:

'Wonder who the bloody hell that is?'

'Looks like Jack – what the hell's he doin' up there?'

'No – can't be Jack. By Jesus, it *is* Jack!'

We lurched to a halt in front of a languid man with an arm half raised in a lazy gesture of 'G'day'.

With unhurried steps this man walked to the side of the train, planted a boot on the running board, leaned in the vehicle and said:

'How yer going, Bill? Bert's sneaking up on a few black duck up ahead on the lagoon, so hold her for a while will yer, Bill?'

We rolled cigarettes and started to yarn until in the distance the faint reports of two shots were heard. Jack took his boot off the train, settled his hat over his eyes.

'She's right, mate. Bert's on to 'em. Yer can take her away.'

A while later Bill pulled up in front of a flimsy bridge. We looked at him questioningly.

Bill merely said, 'Knock open that locker, will yer, and get out them pannikins and that bottle of rum and we'll go down to the crick fer a snort.'

While drinking the rum and water one of us asked Bill if he often stopped like this.

'Or, no,' he said, 'just now and agin. It gives blokes like us a chance to hop down fer a snort and it gives the women a chance to sneak out into the long grass on the other side.'

'But, Bill,' we said, 'there *are* no women on the train.'

Bill said, 'And a bloody good job too!'

6

At Geraldton we drank Swan Lager and ate crayfish from the
Indian Ocean. Then we took the road north and by nightfall we
were camping on the other side of the Murchison River. Next day
we heard the wedgebills calling, and saw the first mallee-fowl of
the trip. The wedgebill's is another melodious voice of the dry
lands. The wedgebill, like the bellbird, is crested, but its outer
tail feathers have white tips. As this recognition mark is soon seen,
the two species can be separated with tolerable ease. Perhaps the
wedgebill, even more than the bellbird, is the characteristic voice
of the mulga. It, too, sings with clear bell-like notes, always from
an eminence, and often by moonlight. Dom Serventy says that
the call sounds like 'Sweet Kitty Lintoff' or, perhaps, even, 'Did
you get drunk?' The song is constantly, even monotonously,
repeated. It begins low and soft. Then it becomes louder and this
gives the impression that the still and hidden bird is floating in
closer towards you.

We saw the lowan or mallee-fowl among eucalypts and acacia
scrub. Mallee is dwarf eucalyptus. The names mallee and lowan
are aboriginal. The mallee-fowl is one of the megapodes or incubator birds. With its big feet, the megapode, generally the male,
works for months scratching together a sandy mound about ten

feet wide. This surrounds a central egg-chamber about three feet deep. Generally an old mound is used, but whether the mound is old or not the central egg-chamber is next filled with dead leaves and later covered with sandy soil. The imprisoned leaves ferment and the egg-chamber gets hot. In the spring the hen lowan begins to lay her disproportionally big pink eggs. Harry Frith, who knows much more about the mallee hen than anybody else, heated their incubators artificially and came to believe that the birds use the tongue as a thermometer in order to test the temperature of the mound. Certainly they probe the mound frequently with their beaks. Then, when the rotting leaves become hotter than is good for the eggs, the birds scratch open the mound early each morning and let the heat escape for a while. In midsummer's heat they pile insulating sand on the mound. This prevents the combination of fermentation and solar heat from destroying the eggs. In the autumn, with the last eggs still in the mound, the heat generated by the ageing leaves is inadequate. Now, during the hottest part of the day, the mound is opened by the birds and the heat of the sun is let *in*!

The female, which expends rather a lot of energy in the production of as many as thirty-three very large eggs between September and February inclusive, does relatively little of the constructional or regulatory labour. Nevertheless she is allowed to do a certain amount of work, but not at critical periods when the internal temperature is in jeopardy. At such times she may be driven off the job by the anxious male.

Normally the mallee-fowl is extremely shy. Yet Frith and his collaborators found that once, fearful that the temperature balance of its incubator was being upset, a male stood fearlessly scratching sand *into* an egg-chamber almost as fast as one of the zoologists experimentally scraped it out!

The incubation period of the lowan is rather more than two months and so eggs will be in the mound until March or even April. Now, in autumn, some birds are already at work refurbishing their incubators in preparation for the next breeding season. Frith says that the breeding season starts when the incubators become sufficiently hot in the spring; and it ends only after they get too cold in autumn. Both male and female work appallingly hard – the male, month after month building and maintaining the mound, and the female, making and laying egg after egg.

When the eggs successfully hatch, the young push up out of the mound and stagger off into the shade to rest. Thereafter they fend for themselves. They have many enemies: dingoes, crows, hawks, goannas and imported foxes all prey on the helpless chicks. That is a reason why, after such sustained egg-laying, the bush is not crammed full of megapodes. Looked at another way, the vulnerability of the babies, with no parental care, is a reason why the adults must go on producing eggs month after month if the species is to survive.

Some have said that mallee-fowl, derived, like all birds, from a reptilian stock, are 'lazy' birds and have retained the reptilian habit of burying their eggs and simply letting rotting vegetation and the sun's rays do the job of incubation. This is absurd. In the first place, they have not 'retained' anything of the sort: their behaviour is grotesquely specialized and is no doubt derived from an avian ancestor that brooded its eggs on the ground like the domestic hen. As for being 'lazy'! Even the most cursory glance at the facts shows that it would be far simpler to build a nest, sit on a clutch of eggs for a while, and have done with the whole business of reproduction until the next year.

Dom, who knows about Western Australian birds, relates in his book that the mallee-fowl makes three sorts of calls: 1. Soft and low, as uttered by the young; 2. Another, like the boom of a pigeon; 3. A third, like 'a human being belching in the throat backwards'.

No such auditory *curiosa* assailed our ears. We saw the odd lowan move quickly across the road into the comfort of the stunted gums and at one camp we saw the wreck of an old mound, but no more. It was near here that we met a bald old gentleman who said that he'd lost his hair 'chasin' girls agin the wind'.

We crossed the Murchison River and pushed north quickly. We had a rendezvous at Onslow with a whale-marking vessel, the *Lancelin*, which was to take us out to Barrow Island and the Monte Bellos. We saw Sharks Bay from afar; Sharks Bay, a Dampier name, later the *Baie des chiens marins* of the Frenchman Baudin. And long before even Dampier, the Dutch had written on this coast the first, and one of the most fascinating, chapters in the history of Australia – a chapter of miscalculation and wreck, mutiny and heroism and murder that has never been adequately told.

Few people outside the country realize that a century or more before 'Captain Cook discovered Australia', numerous Dutchmen had visited and written about this, to them, tragic western coast of the Great South Land. The Dutch captains generally reached the South Land not by choice, but by ill-luck or mismanagement. These seventeenth-century Hollanders were sailing, often with bullion, by way of their rich Cape settlement towards Batavia, the headquarters of the United East India Company. Experience had taught them that it was easier and quicker to sail almost due east from South Africa towards Terra Australis rather than attempt to go directly north-east to the Indies. By so doing they got help from the 'brave west winds' that girdle the earth in the low latitudes, in short, the 'roaring forties'. Often, however, they were driven too far eastward and finished up on the shoals off Western Australia.

Elizabeth of England was dead only thirteen years, and Shakespeare a mere five months, when Dirk Hartog in *Eendracht* made landfall at Sharks Bay (Dirk Hartogzoon Roads). He was followed by a succession of Hollanders who discovered that *rara avis*, the black swan, and who charted parts of the western coast of the Great South Land. *Zeewolf, Wapen van Hoorn, Banda, Batavia* (the scene of mutiny and murder in 1629), *Emeloort, Geelvinck, Nyptangh* and *De Vergulde Draeck* (the *Gilded Dragon*, which foundered between Perth and Geraldton in 1656 with 78,600 golden guilders) were only a few of the ships that reached Australia before Cook's *Endeavour*; and Haevick Claeszoon van Hillegom, Francisco Pelsaert, Piete Dirckszoon, Jan van Roosenbergh, Antonie Caen, Aucke Pieterzoon Joncke, and Willem De Vlaming van Vlielandt were some of the picturesque names that were signed on in them. Few or none of the early Dutchmen seem to have liked this place very much. Many left their bones here.

We crossed the Gascoyne.

We drove through patches of pink parakeelia, we saw blue-and-white wrens with vertical tails, rosy brown Bourke parakeets and crimson chats, and red sandhills, lightly timbered. At Booloogoolooroo we heard the rainbow-coloured bee-eaters calling. We saw many red kangaroos in this country, some of them dead by the roadside after trucks had passed by in the night. At the Lyndon River crossing a black-brown wedge-tailed eagle rested undisturbed. We hoped that he was not a rogue eagle, and would remain unmolested. Just across the Ashburton we saw a couple of big wedge-tails feeding on a dead beast. These great soaring birds are rather bigger than the golden eagle of Europe and were sometimes described as vultures by early travellers. Menzies, naturalist to the 'political' expedition of Vancouver, which called briefly in south-

49

western Australia on the trip from England to show the flag to the Spaniards at Nootka (now called Vancouver), said: 'Of the birds that live in or resort to the woods the vultures may be said to be most common, and we saw several of this species, or at least birds that were so considered.'

The soaring wedgetail does, in fact, rather resemble a vulture at a great distance. Although not rare, it is no longer one of the commonest birds anywhere in Australia. In the past, sheep-farmers persecuted it ruthlessly and arranged that a bounty be put on its head, or rather beak. As long ago as 1892, two shillings per beak was paid by the Western Australian Government, and in 1919 wedgetails were officially declared to be vermin. Between 1929 and 1950 bonuses were paid on more than one hundred thousand beaks. The sheep-farmer of today is, by and large, more educated than his pioneering forebears and he is less likely to grab a gun whenever he sees an eagle. Further, eagles tend to avoid people who carry guns. Today, relatively few farmers believe that all wedgetails are confirmed lamb-killers. There is no doubt that some 'rogue' wedgetails do in fact take lambs when the opportunity is there. Most of them, however, live on carrion. A lot of dead things they take from dingoes, imported foxes, and smaller eagles and hawks. Nowadays fast road traffic kills great numbers of kangaroos by night, and by this means the wedgetail gets many unexpected meals. Even though the wedgetail has a bounty of five shillings on its beak it was pleasant to see that it remains common, and to hear Dom and Ivan Carnaby say that it nests in the Swan Valley within twenty miles of Perth.

The ideal is to strike a balance between the eagle and the sheep-farmer. Both eagle (who was there first) and sheep-farmer have their place in the countryside. The farmer is the more important economically; the eagle the more so aesthetically. The odds now seem to be that in Australia, unlike England, eagle and man will come to terms.

We were now on the cyclone coast. Cyclones come in from the Timor Sea during the monsoon season, sweeping in with greatest frequency between Onslow and Broome. Here the elements are indeed more than fretful as they bid the wind blow the earth into the sea. In 1918 Old Onslow and its jetty were battered by a tearing, roaring cyclone. These are called hurricanes on the Queensland side, and typhoons on the China coast. A new jetty was built at Beadon Point which was thought to be a safer place. The town followed the jetty, except for a few old-timers who refused to uproot themselves. Then, in 1934, the new jetty was smashed. It was rebuilt. Today the two Onslows – 'Old' and new – stand about twenty-five miles apart.

We arrived in Onslow on the right day, but the *Lancelin* was still at sea. So we turned our backs on this dreary little town and went off to camp near a tank in the bush. These life-saving tanks are scattered through the north-west. They have a galvanized iron catchment area (which serves also as a shelter) and this drains into a big tank that gives relief to passing wayfarers. Some have a telephone by which you can call for help. It was here that we met Brumby Bill.

As we went up the north-western coast we became used to the curious names by which men know each other. Take Brumby Bill, for example. A brumby is a wild horse. Brumby Bill is a slightly manic character who appeared in a cloud of dust at our camp near his sheep station. In the back of his latest model car he had a grizzled aboriginal, very sick with pneumonia. Brumby Bill was driving this old abo at speed for about a hundred miles to the nearest hospital because, Brumby Bill reckoned, he could land him there quicker than the local Flying Doctor could get out. After a few cheerful remarks Brumby Bill disappeared in a cloud of dust.

In this country, too, there lived and died The Buck Euro, The Poddy Calf, The Tropical Frog, The Spotted Dog (who all looked rather like these animals) as well as The Whispering Baritone and Treacle Dick (who ate little else).

We met Brandy John. Now an old, old man, he has a long and remarkable history stretching from the colonial days. He started his career as a theological student at one of the senior British universities (Cambridge, no doubt) but a weakness for brandy disrupted his training. So Brandy John went out to 'The Colonies'. (Today Australian families despatch their own black sheep into the friendly anonymity of London.) Brandy John became a sort of remittance man without a remittance. He became tutor (it is said) to the children of one of the late nineteenth-century governors and, later, a master at one of the newly emergent Australian private schools. But brandy (it was always brandy) made it impossible for him to continue in regular employment. He became tutor to the homestead children of outback sheep and cattle stations and, when sober again, a station store-keeper, recording the accounts in meticulous script. He was nearing ninety when we met him, and living at ease. A local store-keeper gives

Brandy John   P—ll Jagoba 61

Brandy John, a graduate of one of the senior universities, Cambridge, no doubt.

Brandy John a rent-free room at the back of his shop. The last sheep station for which he worked pays him one pound a week for old time's sake, and he gets the old age pension. He has become a much respected, if somewhat unsteady, old gentleman in one of the remoter wool ports.

Lancelin arrived during the night. We broke camp at first light and came back to town. While the ship was taking on stores we sorted out the gear needed on the islands and talked to the locals in the Onslow pub.

Nobody who rides the inland or the west can pass up the question of beer, and, in particular, the importance of cold beer. We are a nation of beer drinkers and in the back country little other than beer and rum is drunk. In the cities it is different. There, man's choice is varied as in cities the world over. In Australian cities an enormous amount of good, and some poor wine is drunk. By good wine one does not mean the stuff sent to England in huge stainless steel containers, but good wine by any standards and cheap enough for almost anybody to buy in bulk, and then bottle and drink a glass or two with the evening meal. Ten million Australians drink about the same total quantity of wine as fifty million Britons. There is in Australia, of course, less *bullswool* associated with wine-drinking than in England.

But in the back country, the far north, the land of the Never-Never, in a way of life that offers little comfort and few luxuries, it is cold beer that has the special place; for up there beer is often not too easy to come by, and by the time it reaches you it is apt to be expensive. Beer is the common denominator of sociability and relaxation. In their isolation the blokes feel less isolated. Beer is a great leveller, and it produces a common bond. It is the foundation of a habit, nation wide, that prompts any Australian to call any hotel a pub, whether it be Claridges in London or Moody's at Hall's Creek. In Australia men like their beer cold. The long summers have ingrained this preference, and a great many publicans and homesteads add the refinement of chilling the glasses as well. The Australian in a July heat-wave in London is always appalled at the publican who pumps his luke-warm mild and bitter, and who may even offer to put ice in the glass. It is curious how nations see each other. The British are often disconcerted by certain angularities of the Australian's speech and behaviour, and his frequent inclination to ribald comment on functionaries and institutions that the Englishman is conditioned from childhood to regard as sacrosanct. To the Australian, on the other hand, the Englishman's habit of drinking flat, warm beer is, like his weekly bath and slightly grubby linen, a form of behaviour that exciteth mighty wondering but passeth understanding.

In London there is one publican who sells good strong Australian beer, and cold. This splendid man keeps an outsize refrigerator which he fills with bottles shipped from Melbourne and Perth and he renders expatriates an inestimable service. Such a hero should not go unsung: the pub is The Surrey, and it is in Surrey Street, just off the Strand.

It is easy to understand then, that in the parched areas of the west, where distances are great and the social conviviality of the isolated little tin pubs hard to come by, men in their loneliness will talk longingly around the campfire of memorable nights in the pub, and argue with mock seriousness the virtues of different

Men in their loneliness will talk longingly of memorable nights in the pub.

brands of beer. The Queenslanders and their Bulimba and Castle-maine; the Tasmanians and their lighter Cascades with the red or the green label; the Melbournians with their characterless quartette; the Crow-eaters with their heavy uniquely tangy blue-capped Coopers (though they themselves drink more of a rather inferior thing), the Sand-gropers and their defence of Swan; and even the Sydneysider, with reputedly poor stuff compared with much of the others, will sardonically defend his beer with a loyalty that he would never extend to his tennis players or cricketers.

And how welcome is beer after days of dusty tracks, and sometimes weeks in the saddle. How good to walk out of the glare into the cool and dark interior of the bar, to hoist one's foot on the rail, to lean relaxed against the counter and watch the cold, golden liquid climb the wall of your first glass. There is little talk for a while, an almost solemn moment until, with cigarettes rolled and hats shoved to the back of heads, men look expansively around and begin to ask for news and to yarn. A good moment of comfort, a time to be savoured, much prized, for it only comes once in a while, and there is distance and dust between. These tiny pubs, that may exist by themselves in a wilderness, or form the hub of some small wood and tin township, are the real social centres. In this they resemble those splendid little village pubs of England of which they are mutant forms. Much of the affairs of a district are decided in the bar, livestock is bought and sold, and bargains sealed with a drink. They are labour exchanges as well, for a man looking for work will go to the pub in search of an employer. They disseminate news and mail for they are invariably *poste restante*, and public notices (as we have seen with reference to Whispering Smith) are displayed in the bar.

In an odd way they have even affected the landscape, for on the long leads you will find the inevitable bottles and cans, discarded along the way, where someone has taken, wrapped in wet paper, a few 'cold ones for the road'; a memorial to the drovers' thirst. And of course the pub and cold beer is an excuse to forget for a while the great expanse outside the door, the horizon lost in haze, or the road camp, the out-station, the dogger's hut. There you'll hear all the old yarns, with a new one or two brought in by a stranger. You'll hear of the old no-hoper in The Alice who finally persuaded a store-keeper to let him have a bottle of methylated spirits to drink, but who bitterly complained as he picked it up, 'Fair go, mate, haven't you got a cold one?'

Usually rambling wooden places, verandah'd about, they stand on the plains like ships at sea. Rather shabby, with a coating of summer dust over parched paintwork, with creaking bat-wing doors, a windmill at the back and a tired tree or two, they are the oasis of many a dream. Some are built merely of corrugated iron over trimmed poles cut from the surrounding scrub and paved

Verandah'd about, they stand on the plains like ships at sea.

with termite-mound floors tramped hard like cement. When the weather is warm, and it always seems to be, there will be beds on the verandah, grey-blanketed stretchers. Knick-knacks and mementoes share the shelving with an odd assortment of bottles and a bundle of letters that may wait weeks for claimants. There is little furniture. Furniture is always a scarce commodity in the bar, and what there is usually consists of a couple of battered benches. A drawer beneath the counter is the till, though in some places tobacco tins serve just as well. There is nothing ornate about these places; it is the essentials that matter, and the inessentials slough off into limbo. Like the old clock that may hang on the wall, but never runs. Its entrails long rusted, it may survive for several more generations as a forgotten wedding present for people who had no need of time.

In one such place in the remote north the publican, an elderly giant of a man, put a charge of a shilling a glass on every kind of drink that he had to offer. He explained, simply, that this 'made it easy for addin'.'

There is a story to the effect that one hot summer afternoon while resting on the bed in his 'office', he saw, through a rent in the corrugated iron partition, a stranger helping himself to the contents of the tobacco tins. Broke after a poker game the previous evening, this enterprising gentleman had found a simple way to recoup his losses. He was met on the front verandah by the large bulk of the old publican, who casually looked him over, removed his pipe from his mouth and said, 'Tell you what, mate, I'll go you halves.'

There used to be a pub on a track to nowhere in which nobody seemed to live. The owner had a large spread of sheep country that went with it, and he kept the pub as a service to the termites and the few men who lived scattered about the area. It contained some cases of bottled beer, a kerosene refrigerator and nothing else. On a small bench stood an open meat tin that held assorted change, and there hung above it a bottle opener attached by a piece of string to the wall. Beside the opener was a notice that requested the rare customer to replace in the refrigerator fresh bottles from the cases for any cold ones that he cared to use, to leave his payment in the meat tin, and above all not to 'for Christ's sake, shake [steal] the bloody opener'. The owner only visited the place to refill the refrigerator with beer and kerosene. History has it that nobody did shake that opener.

Not many pubs today keep a drunks' room. This was a room

exclusively reserved for the habituals who hit 'town' once every eighteen months or so with a cheque to cut out. It was used also to house the young sparks from the stations out on a spree after the local bush race meeting. But the old cheque busters usually laid claim to it. They were mostly men who led unbelievably lonely lives maintaining a remote bore pump far out on some station run, or an equally solitary existence such as dogging. The dogger, or dingo hunter, is an almost incredibly skilled bushman who prefers a life of solitude and independence to that of a station hand working for regular wages. The state governments pay a bounty on the scalps that he takes, and if he is unable to cash in his scalps at a police station, he will do so at the store or the pub, counting them out over the bar. These solitary men are usually known as *hatters*. Some of them go under the name of

The Hatter

Randolph Bycroft

The solitary men are usually known as hatters, or death adder men.

death adder men, for it is reckoned they will bite your head off if spoken to before noon. Men who seldom have the chance to talk they become garrulous with their kind and argue endlessly and with great contentment during their rare meetings. On arrival at the pub they would usually go straight to the drunks' room, select a bed from the half dozen stretchers, and throw their swag on it. Then they would enter the bar and hand over their cheque to the publican. Thus they would 'blue' their cheques. The pub-keeper would usually hold back a proportion so as to be able to taper them off the grog and dry them out and get rid of their shakes.

There was never much noise from the drunks' room at night, for the bibulous activities of the day brought exhaustion, and the room would rock instead with the stertorous snoring of the occupants. Accustomed as these men were to waking at daybreak, the pub-keeper would often leave some rum available with which they could warm themselves in the chilly dawn. This was a wise precaution, for if he did not, he was likely to be roused out of bed for a pipe-opener. There was a kind of tacit understanding between publicans and regular cheque busters – a sort of code of tolerance which ensured a surprising minimum of disturbance. Tough and leathery, they would finish their spree, roll their swags, take back their odd left-over cash, load up with tobacco, tea and other necessities, and disappear for another long year or two into the wide landscape whence they had come.

A strange band of characters, they seem to be dying out. Improved and faster means of transport induce men now to spend their leave in the comparative comfort of more populated centres. So many of the younger men today move about their work in jeeps or trucks. And they fly to Perth, or Sydney, or to Europe for their holidays. But the pub still represents home, society and news. A tangible link with an intangible world, where a man can talk to a man and not to his hat. Where arguments abound, and bets are laid, where idiosyncrasy is respected, and where there is found the tolerance and understanding that is given by loneliness to the soul of man.

We have given the impression that the only beverages regularly used in the inland and west are tea and beer. We should not have forgotten rum. Rum is exceedingly important. More of it is consumed in the north of Australia than in any other part of the continent. Of spirits, it is the most popular and properly so, for rum distilled from Queensland cane sugar is very good indeed.

It can be used in a variety of ways: to lace strong tea, to mix with almost any cordial, and it is one spirit which can be drunk with the warm water out of a creek or a stationary water bag, yet still taste right. It warms you in the chill desert nights, and it revives you after long and weary days. Rum has a firm place in Australian history. In the early colonial days it formed an important part of the economy and was used as a form of exchange. The good Governor Macquarie paid with rum the contractors who built the first hospital in Sydney. Rum was the standby of the old pioneers; it followed the coast and rivers and crossed the inland in the saddlebags of the explorers. In the days when transport was limited to ponderous bullock waggons and heavy horsedrawn drays, when space and weight were important and the cost of cartage high, rum was the liquor they carried. Overproof to conserve space, it could be watered down in the tiny bush shanties, slab homesteads and the mining camps of the period. How often you read in the *Journal* of some exploration party penetrating the unknown interior a brief statement that to revive flagging spirits, or to celebrate a goal achieved, 'a tot of grog to all hands' had been issued. Thus, Colonel Egerton Warburton, of whom more later, wrote: 'We camped in the scrub, and have had a treat which few in like circumstances get – rum and fresh milk [of their camels]. I have often abused camels, and persecuted, or rather prosecuted sly grog-sellers. I will never do so again.'

Old Timers of the Kimberleys.   R.D. 61.

They argue endlessly and with great contentment during their rare meetings.

7

We went aboard *Lancelin* next morning and set sail for the isles. None of our party had ever been there before though all of us knew much of them, and perhaps little to their credit, from the literature. From the time of the first Dutchmen, anxious and nostalgic navigators have given this coast a bad name. The French saw nothing romantic in the coastal isles. Baudin's men, in fact, found them 'frightful'. 'In the midst of these numerous islands there is not anything to delight the mind . . . the aspect is altogether the most whimsical and savage . . . this part of New Holland is truly frightful . . . we continued to sail in the midst of shallows and sandbanks, compelled to repeatedly tack, and avoiding one danger only to fall into another.'

We sailed over calm seas. We lunched on heaped plates of king prawns and sliced raw cabbage and tomatoes, and landed on Great Sandy Island before sunset. This is a desolate looking place, yet surrounded by reefs full of small succulent crayfish, stingrays (not in the least succulent) and oysters of respectable size. We hurried ashore in the outboard. We found breeding Caspian terns, sea-eagles and Pacific shearwaters or mutton birds. Mutton birds were so named by the early settlers over in the east who salted their carcases and persuaded themselves that they tasted like sheep.

They do not taste like sheep. Unhappily, they taste exactly like mutton bird despite what Dom Serventy says. They are petrels, with long wings, dark liquid eyes, a tube-nose and dusky, musty-smelling plumage. One of the eastern species makes a mighty migration each year from Tasmania up across the equator to the Aleutians and back, returning to its nesting islands during the same twelve days every year.

The shearwater over whose burrows we tramped is not migratory. It is merely dispersive, moving out across the sea in search of its food of minute floating animals but never going very far from home. We heard them crooning beneath our feet and occasionally stumbled into a burrow. Commander J. Lort Stokes, some-time skipper of the *Beagle*, was troubled by these tunnels on neighbouring islands in 1836. 'The soil,' he said, 'is filled with burrows of the sooty petrel or mutton bird, so that it forms rather troublesome walking.'

A yellow flowering acacia grew plentifully, as well as a trailing vine with purple flowers, and another plant with purple berries. Great Sandy, like all the others in this wide blue sea, is uninhabited but ashore we fell in with a Japanese and two Malay pearl divers. These sturdy little men were all white teeth and smiles. They conversed in the few words of English they had, and told us that their luggers lay off-shore on the other side of the island. They carried long iron rods. These they rammed into the sand. If a rod came up damp it meant that a turtle had laid there. Then they would scoop up the sand and gather a dozen or so reptilian eggs that look like ping-pong balls. We had eaten these in other places. The 'white' does not coagulate with cooking, but the yolks, though a little rank, are not bad if you are really hungry. Turtle steaks, of course, are magnificent. When we topped the low sandy spine of the island we saw two white luggers riding at anchor, glistening in the westering sun. We went back aboard the *Lancelin*, anchored far out, as darkness came. We ate turtle soup and a stew of potatoes and turtle meat.

Our new friends aboard *Lancelin* were Cec Pearce, the skipper, genial and impressively competent; a marine biologist Ray, Mark I, from the Western Australian Museum; Ray, Mark II, a cadet Fisheries Inspector aged seventeen; Roley, a slightly older and rather more studious cadet; and a magnificent swag-bellied man called Tich. On that particular cruise, the main business of *Lancelin* was to mark whales. Tich fired the gun carrying the steel 'dart' on which is engraved a number, a promise of reward, and an address to which information about the size and final locality of the whale should be returned. These men were good company and we talked deep into the night as we lay in our bushmen's swags on the deck under the stars.

There was a lull in our talking when we listened to a broadcast from the other side of the continent by the Melbourne virologist, Macfarlane Burnet. The blokes pricked up their ears when he spoke of the almost certain relationship between cigarette smoking and lung cancer. One of us took snuff reflectively, wondering whether any of the million-odd listeners would be wise enough to take heed and change to snuff (which gives you your nicotine drug without combustion of weed and the evolution of cancer-producing tobacco-tar), or to a pipe or cigar. Burnet's remarks on smoking and lung cancer started a lively discussion. Some years ago one of us had done a little work on the problem and had suggested a possible reason why burning the weed in cigarettes can cause lung cancer, even though burning it in cigars and pipes apparently does not. The report of the work was made in the *British Medical Journal* of May 8th, 1954, but seemingly nobody took any notice of it. This in itself was interesting because in this journal anything that is in the least degree controversial is usually followed by considerable, and often tedious, discussion. A possible explanation was that the general run of suburban 'doctors' who read it failed to understand the physiology of what one was talking about, and the scholarly laboratory professionals and others either declined to read yet another letter headed 'Lung Cancer' or, if they did, they perhaps thought the hypothesis too crazy to bother with. The crew pulled deeply on their cigarettes as the idea was developed in a simplified manner as follows:

Cigarettes, cigars and pipes all produce tobacco-tar, but it is perhaps only from cigarettes that the harmful tar or other by-products cause lung cancer. How, then, does cigarette smoking differ from that of cigars and pipes? Chiefly, in two ways. First, the lighted end of the cigarette is kept closer to the nostrils and smoke is often drawn up into them. Secondly, people who smoke cigarettes inhale more frequently than do pipe or cigar smokers because a series of hearty 'drawbacks' from either pipe or cigar would make most people rather sick. Heavy cigarette smokers, then, get a chronic bronchitis caused by inhalation through mouth, nose, or both. This involves inflammation of the walls of the breathing tubes and a resultant 'weeping' of mucus. This excessive discharge from the irritated respiratory tubes seeps down into the lungs and is coughed up each morning, hence the chronic 'smokers' cough'.

The constant deep inhalation of smoke does all this. Cigarette smokers who do not inhale fumes habitually nevertheless often get smokers' cough because, if they smoke heavily enough, cigarette fumes are drawn up into their nostrils and this too sets up a chronic discharge which seeps into the lungs at night. So it seems that chronic cigarette smokers, whether they habitually inhale or not, and whether they use filter tips or not, will develop a nasty seepage of mucus which penetrates deep into the lungs each night. And this may form a vehicle by which cancer-producing substances from the tobacco-tar, as well as possible cancer-producers floating free in the atmosphere (such as Diesel fumes), can be lodged in the innermost recesses of the lungs of man. But, if you use a cigarette holder that will project the tobacco fumes away from the nostrils, and refrain from the deep oral inhalation of such fumes, then theoretically you should not get lung cancer. It can be predicted that some day in Albania, Bulgaria, Cambodia, Dalmatia or somewhere, there will be found a statistically significant tribal group of holder-users who will prove this most splendid theory right up to the hilt.

The blokes gave all this polite attention, dragging as hard as ever on their smokes. They drew in great lungsfull of tar-laden fumes, and they coughed hoarsely on subsequent mornings. The theoretical biologist continued to take his snuff, wondering whether, tar or no tar, he will perhaps die of cancer of the nasopharynx.

We were up and under way at first light. Then there was a gold glow over towards Australia and suddenly the sun seemed almost to jump over the horizon and spread into a ball of fire.

As we sailed, we fed on thick transverse fillets of Spanish mackerel, gold in colour and as good a fish as was ever eaten by hungry men. Their quality makes nonsense of the oracular declarations by certain fisheries 'experts' that the fishes of warmer waters cannot compare in taste with those of the colder far northern and southern seas. Meanwhile we trolled a bright silver lure, and caught some more. Fishes, though their nervous system (despite silly statements to the contrary) feels pain deeply, are even more stupid than birds, and so they will snap reflexly at anything that flashes silver and resembles the gleaming belly of their habitual prey. The tough sash-cord line had let into it a length of rubber hose-pipe and when this stretched it meant a fish was hooked.

Then there was a quick haul to get the heavy, fighting, flapping game-fish aboard before the sharks got it. Once we did not, and we were left with only the head and the hook.

By 9.30 on the same morning we were off Barrow Island, one of the places on which we wanted to collect. Barrow Island was discovered in June 1818 by Phillip Parker King, out of Sydney, who first sighted the nearby Monte Bello Islands, so named by the Frenchman Baudin a few years earlier. At the same time King found an island outside the Monte Bellos and called it after John Barrow, Esq., one of the Secretaries of the Admiralty.

'We were prevented from steering round it by a very extensive shoal that stretches off its south end towards a low sandy islet which proved to be one that had been seen by us last February. Several attempts were made to find a channel through the reef, but without success; and, at sunset, we anchored to the north-west of the islet, from which several islands were recognised by us . . . as this part of the coast had been previously seen by us, we did not delay any longer, but the following morning steered to the northward.'

One hundred and forty years after King we rounded Double Island and the big colony of pied cormorants that whiten its cliffs. We saw almost 700 of these stream off over the sea and then, on Barrow itself, we found Whitlock Cove, named after a pioneer bird collector who once camped there. This is a wide indentation, partly protected by Double Island and a small headland that became an island at high water. The cove is flanked by a wide but rather dull reef, and is backed by low dunes, hot then in the morning sun. These dunes are covered by stunted acacias and under one of these we pitched a tent. This rapidly became an oven, but it would keep our scales and specimens safe from wind-blown sand. Soon we got into a routine of working in the sparse shade of the acacias. We cooked and slept in the open, about forty yards down-slope where the spinifex met the beach.

Nearby we found the eggs of a pied oystercatcher lying in a scrape on the ground. Dampier, too, found it on this coast in 1699. He called it 'the crabcatcher'. 'The Bill and Leggs of this Bird are of a Bright Red,' Dampier wrote. The two most notable inhabitants of Barrow are the spinifex bird and the black-and-white wren. The brown spinifex bird, relatively rare on the mainland, is common. It is a vivacious, liquid-voiced bird with a long wedge tail. It says *je suis à vous!* It chatters engagingly from the top of any clump of bushes or spinifex in its territory, and is very easy to see. Surprisingly, it remained undiscovered until 1900.

The petite black-and-white wren is different in almost every way. Man towers above the spinifex and can be seen hundreds of yards away. Shy and elusively fast, the little pied wren could be seen only as a brief flash as it darted close to the ground from clump to clump, sometimes travelling fifty yards in a headlong dash. Then it would disappear. It was only when we deserted the spinifex and reached the long dry river bed, full of tall blue-flowering shrubs (where we found a nest and eggs), that the tables were turned. Here the little black-and-white wrens, and their brown females, had to get up into the vegetation to see the man. This river was named the Donald, in honour of a very small boy in Hampstead who had presented one of us with the notebook in which some of this was originally scribbled. Its dry bed was followed down to the coast where it found a mangrove swamp in which there lived a sacred kingfisher, a bird new to the island list.

Historically, too, the lovely little black-and-white wren is interesting. It was first discovered and collected on neighbouring Dirk Hartog Island by the French naturalists Quoy and Gaimard who sailed these coasts in 1818 in de Freycinet's *Uranie*, out of Toulon. *Uranie* was later wrecked. The skins of the little wrens were lost and so the species was officially named and described *in absentia*. The female, like those of most of the Australian fairy-wrens, is a dainty brown, but the male is a glory. He is velvet black except for his silky white shoulders. This is an island race, known only from here and Dirk Hartog about 350 miles away. The other race is the blue-and-white wren, which has an immense continental range. In this species the black of the body and wings is replaced by vivid blue.

The only likely explanation of the curious difference between mainland and island races is that in the far distant past the parent mainland stock was somehow geographically separated into two elements. This would allow the species to differentiate into a blue-and-white interior race and a black-and-white coastal race. Then, the black-and-white coastal race spread to the islands offshore. Next, the blue-and-white interior race spread westward and swamped the black-and-white birds (but not the isolated islanders) by interbreeding. Odd coastal birds have been collected that were almost as black as blue. The mainland stock is nowadays essentially blue-and-white, but the genetic integrity of the island birds is protected by their isolation.

Meanwhile, Ivan, the ex-kangaroo shooter, was out after hare wallabies and the euro. It was strange to reflect that the graceful little hare wallaby was discovered on this wild coast as early as 1699. Dampier landed at Sharks Bay, a little to the south of where we now were, and on August 6th killed 'a sort of Raccoon . . . with very short Forelegs' and found it to be 'very good meat'.

At night, bandicoots, sharp-nosed little insect-hunters, foraged around our camp and were held in the rays of our flashlights. They came around us all night and burrowed for beetles in our tent, as their ancestors had done in Whitlock's forty years before. There were native rodents too; and in a dwarf tree Ken Buller found a most exciting little marsupial allied to the savage native 'cats' of the mainland. One of the big wallabies – the euro – had a minute joey in her pouch.

It was a tiny naked and blind baby and, attached as it was to the nipple, one could easily understand how men for three centuries had believed – as some still believe – that young marsupials grow out of the nipples and are 'born in the pouch'.

The first marsupials described were those of North and South America. At one time, as proved by fossilized bones, marsupials were common in many parts of the earth. As time went on they were beaten in competition by the more 'progressive' (a splendid zoological cliché) mammals which evolved, among other modern attributes, a placenta. That is to say, there arose in them a filter between womb-wall and the attached unborn young one. This new device enabled the babe to be carried protected within the body of the mother and to be at the same time fed by the food and oxygen circulating in her blood. So the young one had time to develop to a degree that gave it a better chance of survival. Rats and bats, and dogs and cats and man are all placental mammals.

In most marsupials no such efficient filtering device has arisen; and so the young are born after a few weeks' gestation period and in a correspondingly undeveloped condition. When first born, the young of a six-foot boomer kangaroo is less than an inch and a half long. It is naked, blind and helpless. But it is born by the same route as is man. By means of an astounding series of reflexes (instincts), the blind and still partly transparent babe 'swims' upwards through the mother's fur, drops into her pouch and attaches its tube-like mouth to a nipple. The nipple swells inside the baby's mouth as the milk is extracted.

If anything more violent than the gentlest traction is used in the removal of the pouch baby, its tiny mouth ruptures and bleeds. So arose the legends that the young of marsupials are born through the nipples. A few white people – even including some professional kangaroo shooters – believe this in Australia today, even though it is easy for them to dissect an embryo out of the uterus during the sexual season.

The reason why Australia and New Guinea remain a stronghold of the marsupials is that these countries have been separated from the northern parts of the world for many millions of years, and this isolation has given the ancient local fauna protection from the placental creatures that arose later and conquered the north. South America, in the past often separated from the north, has remained a second stronghold. One marsupial, the ugly but edible Virginian opossum, has withstood modern competition in the south-eastern United States.

As the sixteenth- and seventeenth-century voyageurs explored the Americas, a fantastic collection of legends arose concerning the birth of marsupials. Thus, Peter Martyr, a Venetian courtier, wrote in the early sixteenth century of 'beastes', the female of which bore 'her whelpes abowte with her in an outwarde bellye much lyke unto a greate bagge or purse'. In the seventeenth century, a Dutch physician, Piso, claimed that 'the pouch is the uterus . . . it has no other, as I have determined by dissection. Into this pouch the semen is received and the young form therein.'

Soon pioneer settlers in the English colony of Virginia became familiar with the local marsupial. Apparently the Red 'Indian' name was possum, preceded by a grunt which was responsible for the prefixed 'o'. 'An Opossum . . . is of the bigness of a Cat. Under her belly she hath a bagge, wherein shee lodgeth, carrieth, and sucketh her young,' wrote Captain John Smith in 1608. It was natural that the uneducated settlers and convicts in Virginia should come to think that 'these creatures are bred at the Teats by the Dams' but, almost as soon, a Dr Tyson found by dissection 'that their Structure is formed for Generation like that of any other Animals' and that they must necessarily be 'bred and excluded the usual Way of other Quadrupeds . . .' The scientist Catesby, however, reported, that 'by what Method the Dam after Exclusion fixes them to her teats is a Secret yet unknown'.

One old North American belief was that opossums copulate through the nose and that, after a while, the minute young are somehow squeezed into the pouch. Hartman, the authority on American marsupials, has suggested that the possession by marsupials of a bifid penis has something to do with this particular legend. The twin apertures of the nasal region, too, are obvious; whereas the twin internal genital arrangements of the female opossum are not. Hartman has gathered other fables which hold the opossums 'Ingender at the Ear and bring forth their young at the Mouth'. One Texas frontiersman wrote that the opossum delivers its young direct from the womb into the pocket *through* the old 'teet'. The little fellow, he claimed, brings the new 'teet' with it in its mouth. This it never turns loose while it stays in the pouch. 'The borning process is very slow,' said the man from Texas, and when the young get too big for the pouch 'they are borned again into the wide world'.

The first Australian marsupial was described by Pelsaert whose ship *Batavia* was wrecked not far south of our present camp about 300 years ago. 'We found on these strands large numbers of a species of cat, which are very strange creatures; they are about the size of a hare, the head resembling that of a civet cat; the forepaws are very short, about the length of a finger, on which the animal has five small nails or fingers, resembling those of a monkey's forepaw. Its two hind legs, on the contrary, are upwards half an ell in length, and it walks on these only, on the flat of the heavy part of the leg, so that it does not run fast. Its tail is very long, like that of a long-legged monkey; if it eats, it sits on its hind legs and clutches its food with its forepaws, just like a squirrel or monkey.

'Their manner of generation or procreation is exceedingly strange and highly worth observing. Below the belly the female carries a pouch, into which you may put your hands; inside this pouch are her nipples, and we have found that the young ones grow up in this pouch with the nipples in their mouths. We have seen some young ones lying there, which were only the size of a bean, though at the same time perfectly proportioned, so that it seems certain that they grow there out of the nipples of the mammae, from which they draw their food, until they are grown up and are able to walk. Still they keep creeping into the pouch with them when they are hunted.'

So, at about the same time as the early American travellers were affirming that the young were formed on the nipples, a Dutch navigator at the other side of the world fell into the same understandable error. Pelsaert was observing the Tammar or Dama Wallaby. It was not until 1817 that this animal was described in scientific terms.

The birth of a marsupial was authentically recorded at least as early as 1830 when an officer in H.M.S. *Success* saw a joey born *per vaginum* from a captive mother kangaroo, and, moreover, saw it crawl through the reclining doe's fur towards her pouch 'as expeditiously as a snail'. As early as 1847 a North American physician, Middleton Michael, observed the birth, *per vaginum*, of an opossum. Since then marsupial birth – American opossum and Australian koala and kangaroo – has been described many times. In the koala and some species of opossums and phalangers the tiny young make the journey from vulva to pouch unaided. In at least some species of kangaroos, the doe licks a pathway through her fur for the young one to follow. One report says that the doe holds the pouch open for the reception of the advancing joey.

There were small black ants in millions on Barrow Island but they caused no real trouble. Our only major complaint was the kangaroo ticks. They seemed to inhabit every bush. They dropped down on us, and imperceptibly bored into our hides. Then we would itch, and gently prise them off so as not to leave their heads in our flesh. But we rarely found them before they had injected into us a capsule of irritant and this, for those who were not used to it, meant intermittent itching and scratching for months after the trip was over.

By beach and reef and mangrove creek, the big green turtles allowed themselves to be stranded by the ebb of the tide. We did not molest them. On these uninhabited isles they have no enemies apart from the odd marauding pearler in search of meat and eggs. So they were contemptuous of danger, and if we sat on the hard hummock of their carapace they merely opened rheumy eyes, and then slowly closed them again. Those already half-submerged in the sea would scull, with blunt heads popping up, leisurely away from us. Every rock was heavily encrusted with oysters. This overcrowding did not make for size, but a meal could be got quickly enough simply by fracturing the shells with any handy piece of rock. So we ate oysters, the liver and the chops of euros, and some of the food we had bought ashore. On cloudless days the sun was savage from 11 until 4 o'clock, and we drank a lot from the cans we had carried off from the *Lancelin*. There is no permanent water ashore. The wild creatures that cannot synthesize their own water must make do with what they get from their feed and the evening dews. Like that of most inlands, the fauna is restricted to few species because there are relatively few ecological niches. And most of the species that have made a foothold have been able to flourish mightily, and become far more common here than they could on the neighbouring continent.

We saw an immense pile of sticks, visible half a mile away. The sticks were formed into a nest on a low dead tree on the low ridge above the shore. This was an osprey's nest. It contained a big chick which the parents fed while we watched. These birds were one of the species most frequently seen by the early explorers. As early as 1697, De Vlaming's people 'found some Birds nests of a prodigious greatness, so that Six Men could not, by reaching out their Arms, encompass One of them; but the Fowl was not to be found'. A French surgeon-naturalist of the *Uranie* found a nest and eggs in September 1818. He called the bird a 'white bellied goshawk with grey back'. After living in England, where the onslaughts of egg-collectors and sportsmen scarcely allow ospreys to exist, it was pleasant to see them here and on the mainland very close to large towns.

Lowendal Island was next, and then others; more islands than we have time to write about. We landed on clean sandy beaches, walked over areas of turf pitted with the burrows of mutton birds that crooned in the darkness beneath our feet. We did the job we came to do and went back aboard, leaving small trace of our fleeting visit. We knew not how many people had visited these uninhabited isles before us. We knew which scientists had been there, for their rare visits are lengthily recorded in the literature. Some broken, green-black, square-faced gin bottles of the Victorian period, and once the ancient remains of a pearler's hut, were evidence of longer stays than ours. On another island we found some beer bottles, probably Edwardian ones, of a different coloured glass from that used today. And on one of the Monte Bellos a whole hillside, scorched by the incredible blow-lamp of an atom bomb, testified to the most recent visitation by man. Here we found modern English beer bottles. We discussed these matters at some length. We concluded that various *culture periods* could be deduced from the bottles and the activities of the gentlemen who drank from them.

On previous voyages through this ocean we had often seen whales in the blue distance. Now, perhaps, was an opportunity to see one of the big plunging humpbacks at close quarters. But the *Lancelin* had finished her marking programme. Ship and crew were prolonging their stay at sea only to allow us to visit the islands. Had the Western Australian government, and the crew, not been so uncommonly obliging, we would never have left Onslow. Would they take the further trouble to find us a whale?

Cec, the skipper, said we might still manage to find one or two moving down the coast on their migration into the cold seas of the south.

We told Ray, Mark II, the Rabelaisian seventeen-year-old who usually manned the masthead, that if he found us a whale we would most assuredly buy him an excessively large bottle of beer when we got back to Onslow.

'Don't drink,' he said.

'All right, fifty cigarettes.'

'Don't smoke,' he said.

'Well,' (as a last resort) '. . . a woman.'

'*Now*, yer talken!' he yelled, and with wild enthusiasm disappeared into the rigging like a rat up a rope.

For an hour Ray, Mark II, kept shouting down that no whale in the mighty Indian Ocean would escape his osprey's eye and, sure enongh, at length there came the exultant yell, '*Thar she blows!*' a sound strange to hear in the mid-twentieth century.

And surely, dead ahead, was a frothy steamy spout. Soon the kid reported that it was a big cow, a forty-foot cow, with calf close alongside. She was not yet on migration, the skipper said, but just heaving about with her calf and about to go.

We got out our movie camera. Tich hitched his shorts up near his belly. Then he climbed with his shotgun into the crow's nest mounted over the bows of the plunging ship. He loaded his gun with a shot cartridge from which projected an eleven-inch steel dart. Now he stood balanced, at the ready.

Ray, Mark II, clung like a possum to the rigging. He watched the cow and calf sound, calculating where they would surface to blow and breathe. With a fascinating stream of obscenity he directed the wheelhouse to manoeuvre port or starboard. Ship and cow and calf pitched onwards. The little one kept an exact distance from his imperturbable dam. The kid in the rigging exhorted the gunman not to waste time, to get a wriggle on, to wake up, to remove the digit, not to go to sleep, to get cracking, and not to behave like an old moll at a christening. There was a series of sharp explosions. Soon the cow had two darts in her thick insulating coat of blubber, and the calf one. The big cow would roll on, south and north, north and south, until she fell prey to the explosive-headed harpoon of an Australian, British, Japanese, Norwegian or Russian. She would yield the board of directors, or their equivalent, eight tons of oil at £90 per ton.

Lancelin turned sharply for the coast of Australia and the terrible infant swung triumphantly down out of the rigging.

'Told yer I'd get yer one.'

'Yes. Thank you very much indeed. What sort of woman do you want – dark, blonde or a red one.'

'Don't care.'

'A big one, or a little one?'

'Don't care.'

'An old one, or a young one?'

'*What!* Fair go! A young one, of course. Yer don't think I want an old crow of twenty-five?'

8

We said goodbye to the *Lancelin* at Onslow and started off north towards Broome and the Kimberleys where we would meet the other party. From here onwards we would be without the services of Ken Buller who must return to his job at the Western Australian Museum. Ken originally came from Warwickshire, 'where all the castles are'. We were sorry to be without his cheerful company and quiet professional competence as he prepared specimens in the flickering half-light of campfires and, latterly, on the rolling deck of the *Lancelin*.

We passed Peedamulla Station, and Warranboo and Yarraloola. These are good names, and we rolled them, and many more, appreciatively across our tongues. We said: Adamin·aby, Jin·dabyne, Tum·barum·ba, Ger·ringong, Yak·andan·dah, Nim·itabel, Jeril·derie, Wooll·oomooloo·, Bithon·gabel, Narran·dera, Narre War·ren, Euran·geline. Perhaps (as some foreigners have said) you have to be at least third generation Australian fully to appreciate this music. We talked, too, of former camps at Leather Barrel Creek, Jew's Pinch and Hopping Dick Creek, just below Bithongabel. This creek, and the tiny settlement of Limpinwood, are supposed to be named after an afflicted gentleman called Richard Wood who once lived there.

Now we were crossing relatively flat country of recent age, land that was even younger than the isles through which we had sailed on shallow seas a few days before. In sharp transition we could see the distant Hamersley Ranges, a tumbled and rugged tableland made of rocks laid down in a Protozoic sea, perhaps a thousand million years ago. Great blocks of Western and Northern Australia, and long tongues of country elsewhere, are so formed and this has given rise to a silly local belief that Australia is the 'oldest country in the world'. Australia is no older than any other continent. It is, however, a stable, rigid shield, and much of it has altered relatively little since the days when life first appeared on earth.

That afternoon we pulled in at Mardie Station. The owner, R. B. Sharp, said that beds would not do us any harm for just one night. Sharp is an old infantry digger with an acute and informed interest in natural history. Even Ivan, who hates all officers (also ticks, policemen, yanks, eyties, snakes, and fleas) thought he was not a bad sort of a bloke. Sharp mentioned casually that 'bronzewing pigeons' had appeared in phenomenal numbers this year and were of a kind that had not been seen on the station in living memory.

We pricked up our ears. There are several bronzewinged pigeons in Australia and two of them are common enough to have been mentioned by many of the early explorers. A bronzewing pigeon was perhaps the first land-bird ever recorded in Australia, for Pelsaert, wrecked on Houtman's Abrolhos in June 1629, wrote of 'grey turtle doves', which may have been bronzewings. Dampier, too, ate 'small turtle doves, that are plump, fat and very good meat'. In 1792 Labillardiere 'killed the charming yellow turtle dove, remarkable for six or eight golden feathers towards the base of its wings'. This was the brush bronzewing. In 1818 Quoy had written of 'turtle doves with metallic sheen', and the overlander Warburton, of whom a little more in a minute or so, had, not very far from here, eaten them in 1872-3. He wrote in eulogistic testimony of 'a plump, heavy bird, weighing, when in good condition, nearly a pound; and its pectoral muscles being deep and fleshy it constitutes a most excellent viand and is constantly eaten by every class of persons, being equally acceptable at the table of the Governor and at that of the inmate of a log hut. . . .'

We, too, had eaten them in various places; with due care, however, because a feed of bronzewing is sometimes not without hazard for the unwary. Bronzewings relish the seeds of the box-poison plant, *Gastrolobium*. The birds have themselves developed over the ages an immunity but, instead of being wholly detoxicated by the liver, at least some of the poison seems to be stored in their bones. The flesh of the bronzewing, then, is safe and good to eat. But, if the bones are chewed, there is great danger. Dogs that eat discarded bones or entrails suffer convulsions, 'go mad', and may bite savagely before they die.

Neither of the two familiar bronzewings fly in big flocks. So, when the owner of Mardie spoke of *numbers* of bronzewings suddenly appearing as a 'new' bird on the station, it seemed that this might be a zoological event of the century and that he was describing the harlequin bronzewing, or flock pigeon. This bird was one as stupendously common as was the now extinct American passenger pigeon, and it, too, declined mysteriously and was thought to be on the verge of extinction.

Sharp said the pigeons had come in about six months ago. The station aborigines did not know what they were. First, a couple of hundred came to the Robe River to water, and now plenty came each day to drink at the Mardie Pool not far from the station homestead.

We were out to the pool in almost no time at all. As the sun sank we saw flock after flock, from ten to sixty birds in each, come in from the dry south-west and circle over the still waters. Successively the flights came in, either dipping directly down to the shallow water or alighting on the nearby shore. The birds stayed only for a few seconds. We counted at least one thousand before the waves ceased some ten minutes before sunset. We made a colour movie film of them. Then we took just one specimen for a skin to make absolutely sure of identification. It was remarkable to see an animal with which we were familiar only from the literature and the colour plates of Gould and Mathews, and which none of us had ever really hoped to see in life.

The bird we collected was a harmony of blue-grey, cinnamon, black, white and metallic purple. We showed the fresh skin to the station aborigines. Old Alec now said that he had, in fact, seen them as a boy, the last one on the Gascoyne about thirty-five years ago. Parrot thought that he had seen a few up the Robe River about ten years before. None of the younger aborigines had known of their existence.

We were up before daybreak and reached the Pool again in the first light. It was good to see flocks of budgerygahs one hundred strong sweep down to drink, hastily dip their beaks, and fly up and off with an unusual clatter. But only one stray flock pigeon came again before sun-up and two a little after.

Once we were on the road again we had time to look up the scanty literature we carried, and we tried to remember what we had read in the past about the flock pigeon. Most early collectors had used phrases such as 'immense flocks', 'multitudes' or even 'countless myriads'. In 1861 John McDouall Stuart, the first man to cross the continent, saw them converge on waterholes in 'clouds'. In 1901 Tom Carter likened the roar of their wings to the noise of surf on a reef, and in 1864 Kendric Bennett said that when a vast flock simultaneously took flight the noise resembled thunder, and that they 'darkened the air' as they wheeled in again to land. Macgillivray, at about the turn of the century, found 'countless mobs' in the Gulf Country where the aborigines simply knocked them down with sticks when they wanted meat. Sometimes the birds almost hid the ground, and they laid eggs in thousands 'all over the plain'. Two white eggs were put in each 'nest', which is just a small scrape under a salt-bush or tuft of grass.

Other people have told of sheep camping in nesting areas and walking away in the morning with the yellow yolks, and the white shells, clinging to their woolly hides. From Gould's discovery of the bird in 1839 until the turn of the century, the story was almost always the same – the sudden and unpredictable invasion of millions of grass-land nomads into an area that rain had made freshly green. But, by 1908, travellers were reporting only 'a few'. Nobody knew what appalling disaster had struck the whole vast population in so short a time. There is a tendency, often a just one, to blame shooters for the decline of a species. Of course, many flock pigeons were shot. One traveller in 1886 bagged forty-two with a single murderous discharge. But even this sort of shooting made little difference to their numbers. The ecological factors responsible for their decline are subtle ones about which, at present, we can hardly even guess. They are seed-eaters, and there is little doubt that overstocking by 'hungry' sheep-farmers not only spoiled their pastures by preventing the grass from seeding but also ruined favourite feeding areas by erosion. Yet these factors alone cannot explain the disappearance of the flock pigeon from almost the whole vast area of the continent over which it roamed. If some wide-spread factor repeatedly deprived the flock pigeon of the opportunity to reproduce, the species would quickly wane. Otherwise, the obvious, but merely hypothetical, explanation is that some frightful pandemic hit the species and laid it low.

The wonderful thing is that it seems to be recovering. In 1929 a flock of sixteen were seen near Onslow, and a little before our encounter a museum party saw several groups of about thirty birds each in the Hamersleys. Although we did not know about it, in the same year that we saw them at Mardie, other flocks of 400 to 500 were seen in the Onslow area, and since then, several people have seen small parties of birds at water-holes here and there. All the evidence seems to suggest that *Histriophaps histrionica* is on the way back when we all feared that it was just 'hanging on' before suffering the fate of the dodo, the great auk and the passenger pigeon.[1] The skin of the single bird we shot was preserved with far more than ordinary care. At our next camp we ate the small muscular body with due ceremony; after all, we must have been among the few living persons who had ever tasted one.

As we passed through the station country we asked men whether they had heard of the green-and-yellow night parrot. This is a desert bird that leaves the shelter of the spiky spinifex tussocks only after nightfall. It drinks at remote water-holes in the dead of night. Even when it was still plentiful, the night parrot was rarely seen by white man. Some people told us they had heard of it, but on each such occasion we soon satisfied ourselves that they were confusing it with the pretty little rosy-brown Bourke parrot, a day-flier which nevertheless prefers to drink just after nightfall, and before the first streaks of day. We saw many Bourke parrots. Although this species, too, became relatively rare after the introduction of sheep and rabbits it is now slowly gaining in numbers and seems out of danger. We saw it often.

Unfortunately, there is no such optimism regarding the night parrot. We carried with us the battered skin of a swamp parrot – a bird that looks not unlike the night bird we wanted to find. This skin we showed to many men and women, including aborigines, on the outback stations. None had seen it.

The night parrot was discovered in spinifex breakaway country near Mount Murchison in 1854, and was seen fairly often between 1875 and 1885. Since then there have been a few reported sightings, but it is possible that no white man has seen the bird for

[1] It *is* on the way back! Several flocks have been seen since this was written.

the past thirty years. However, if the Bourke parrot, and the flock pigeon are 'coming back' perhaps – just perhaps – this gives hope for a similar revival of the night parrot, if it has not already gone forever.

The causes of the decline of the night parrot are obscure. Shooters had nothing to do with it because nobody, except odd zoological collectors, was ever acutely aware of it. An as yet unrecognized combination of harmful conditions imposed by the presence of domestic stock or rabbits is a vague theory. Yet the night parrot lived mostly in the heart of the spinifex desert, far from the maleficial influences of the European. This ability to live in virgin desert makes its sudden disappearance all the more difficult to understand.

We crossed the Fortescue, a river that rises east of the dissected wilderness of the Hamersleys. We reached Roebourne, a settlement graced by several fine old stone buildings made in the convict days but which has unhappily been allowed to degenerate into a slightly sordid little township, with hardly a tree in the place. Yet Roebourne stands beside a pleasant pool on the Harding River, a pretty stream named after a pioneer who was speared by the aborigines. We drank good Swan beer at Roebourne. Then we got out of the place as fast as we could along a rough and washed-out bush track to Cossack, an abandoned pearlers' port that lay deserted, fairly sizzling in the noontide heat.

Cossack is a ghost town. It is full of charm and character. A wharf remains, as well as several stone buildings including a quite magnificent convict-built courthouse, lofty and cool inside, and with its bench still intact. How good if one could transplant this building elsewhere; what a glorious small country house it could make! It was here, too, that we saw the first masses of Sturt's desert pea sprawling red over the parched earth. From the reefs off Cossack were once gathered a great harvest of sea pearls and, from its hinterland, gold and, it is said, sandalwood, were shipped direct to the outside world. The scented sandalwood was sent north to the Orient.

From the dawn of history, timber from trees of the genus *Santalum* has given fragrant oils for the making of perfumes and medicines and joss-sticks; pastes for caste-marks; and small items such as fans and boxes. The slim Western Australian tree grows to about eighteen feet high. It was soon discovered to be a valuable source of revenue for, as early as 1845, the first four tons were exported from the Swan River settlement and since then thousands of tons have been cut, stripped and sent away from south-western ports. Near the coast the sandalwood tree has become relatively rare, but it thrives in the low rainfall areas farther inland and is in no danger of extinction.

It was out from Cossack, then a bustling pearling town, that the reputedly unique Southern Cross of pearls was found in the eighties of the last century. The shell was gathered off Baldwin's Creek, in Carnot Bay, but it was not opened until the schooner *Ethel* reached the skipper's home in the Lacepede Islands. Local legend says that the schooner was wrecked, but that her crew got ashore in the night. Clarke, the lad who had actually found the pearls in their shell, is said to have swam back to the wreck next morning and retrieved them, and a bottle of square-face gin for good measure. The Cross is about one and a half inches long and is formed by a group of large adherent pearls of which seven make up the central shaft, and one on each side the cross-piece. Many people have said that the Cross is a fake. They rudely held it was fabricated by joining individual pearls together. However, Saville Kent says that when the Cross was taken to London for the Colonial and Indian Exhibition of 1886 it 'withstood the severest tests applied, and it emerged from the ordeal with the added lustre of high scientific testimony as to its *bona fide*'.

Nevertheless, a number of sceptics still persisted in the story that the Cross is fraudulent. Taunton, who wandered about these coasts, states that 'Shiner' Kelly, who commanded the *Ethel*, certified in a local newspaper (title not stated) that the Cross was in three pieces when it was found. If this report is genuine, the inference is that 'Shiner', otherwise James William Sherbrook Kelly, was at least mildly annoyed. First, it had been publicly stated that, when the shell was opened, both Kelly and Clarke were 'filled with awe and amazement', that Kelly had regarded the Cross as a 'heaven sent' miracle and, in an excess of Hibernian superstition, had buried it for a period before he brought it to the open market.

There was, too, the implication that Mr Kelly was secondarily annoyed because, as he allegedly states, the Cross was not a cross when his employee, Clarke, handed it to him March 26th, 1883, but was in three distinct pieces. However, he admits that Clarke told him that it was perfectly cruciform when its housing shell was prised open. Kelly's supposed account says nothing of the wreck, nor of the romantic swim through the swell for the Cross and the bottle of gin. Kelly says that he sold the pieces to another pearler, Frank Roy, for £10, who sold them to a gentleman called Frank Craig for £40. Craig in turn sold the pearls to a syndicate for an unnamed sum. The newspaper letter attributed to Kelly is rounded off with an acid statement that the writer now has no interest in the 'object'.

By then, the pearls that Kelly had sold for £10 were valued by a syndicate at £10,000. It is a fair inference that Mr Kelly was feeling a little put out, and perhaps doubly so in view of the rumours that he had superstitiously buried the pearls. Nevertheless, it will be seen that although Shiner Kelly said they were in three pieces when first shown to him, he did not suggest that the pieces could not together form a 'perfect cross'.

By 1903 Henry Taunton, in his book *Australind*, was hot on the trails of Kelly for the suppression of a 'truth', and some person or persons unknown for the fabrication of the Cross. Taunton says bluntly that Kelly's three fragments did not together make up a complete cross, but instead, they formed merely an object that lacked the right arm. This was a fact, said Taunton darkly, that 'strangely enough Kelly seems to have forgotten to mention'.

The participants in this nacreous drama are all dead many years gone and perhaps truth never will out. Was Mr Taunton not over-subtly suggesting that the silence of Mr Kelly had been bought by the syndicate that was now preparing to sell the Southern Cross for £10,000?

Taunton says that he, too, touched at the Lacepedes soon after the pieces were found. When Frank Roy (who bought them for £10) showed him the three pieces they still wanted a single pearl to form a cross. Taunton said that the original pieces were afterwards joined by diamond cement, and that the Cross was still incomplete when it was sold at Cossack at the end of the season of 1882-3.

'As if to assist in the deception, nature had fashioned a hollow in the side of the central pearl just where the added pearl would have to be fitted . . .

'The whole pearling fleet with their shells and pearls [were] coming into Cossack about this time – it was no difficult matter to select a pearl of the right size and with the convexity required.

'The holder paid some ten or twelve pounds for the option of selecting a pearl within given limits; and then, once more with the aid of diamond cement and that of a skilful faker, this celebrated gem was at length transformed into a perfect cross.

'Of the pearl's history after it left Cossack,' concluded Taunton, 'nothing is known by myself.'

When the Southern Cross was taken to Europe, nobody seemed keen to buy it for £10,000. One would have thought that it would have been offered to Royalty, and graciously accepted, but the colonials took it back home instead. In Perth, Saville Kent enjoyed the privilege of the possession of 'this wondrous Cross' for two whole days and nights, in order that he might examine, and (as he said) immortalize, it with his camera. Saville Kent reported that he found the responsibility of sleeping with the equivalent of £10,000 under his pillow 'nerve-stirring'. Such a responsibility, he said, would not have been as 'lightly undertaken, and probably not as promptly conceded, in London as in the as yet unsophisticated capital of Western Australia'. How very right he was.

We talked of these things, and wondered where now was the 'wondrous Cross', as we walked about the abandoned town.

Cossack brooding, deserted in the tropical heat, reminded us of another ghost town, Ebagoola, visited on Cape York Peninsula during the war.

We first heard about Ebagoola from Micky, an ancient prospector who had been on the Peninsula for ages. Micky had a humped back, but it didn't hamper him in his scrabbling for gold and tin in the creek beds. He lived in a rough shelter that he built himself on the creek bank beneath the massive droopy-leaved paper-barks. The creek was dry when we came by but there was cool water under the sands. In the sand of the creek bed, Micky had sunk a well with kerosene tin sides to stop the sand from falling in. When the summer floods swept over the north his well would be ruined, Micky said. But it didn't matter because he wouldn't need a well then. In Micky's shanty were two rusty guns. One was a ·38 Winchester bound up with copper wire. The other was a rusty double-barrelled shotgun that Micky said worked all right.

One of us was the O.C. a Long Range Reconnaissance Patrol during the early dark days of the Japanese invasion of nearby New Guinea when we met Micky. He told us about the country ahead, with a great deal of spitting and swearing. He was a great hand at drawing in the sand with a stick. Micky had much information that was useful to us, but in order to get it you had

Micky had much information that was useful to us.

to question him as carefully as you would a myall. This does not mean that Micky was stupid. It was merely that he and the other Peninsula folk have a scale of time different from ours. For instance, a load of machinery taken along our route 'not long ago' really went (one learnt after questioning) eighteen years before, when the road was last trafficable to the teamsters. An event which occurred in 1908 was 'a fair while ago'. Here men's memories are long and accurate: they have nothing much else to think about apart from their neighbours and their personal experiences among the hills. Micky's sole hell was the toothache. A couple of his teeth were 'not too good'.

'You haven't got a fang-farrier with you, have you?' he asked us, looking at the lounging troops. We hadn't.

So Micky said he'd go down to Normanton 'some day'.

That is how we heard about Ebagoola. The convoy once more took to the bush. The leading drivers picked out an old, old trail along the sandy ridges covered with ironbark, and other gums with round shiny leaves. About fifteen miles to the west we could see a mountain range in territory shown blank white on our maps. We dragged through a sombre land of umbers and olives where termite architecture rose twelve feet between the trees. The drivers often found it hard to get their big blitz-buggies between the trees and the termite-hills.

Three days later we came to Ebagoola. Once it was like any other Peninsula settlement, but the mineral had cut out and the people had walked away from their homes and possessions. On a corner of the two principal streets you could see the remains of the inevitable wide-verandah'd pub. In the wide main street was the butcher's shop and next door, the general store. There were the ruins of a dance hall, more shops, and houses. Then we met Old Ted and we talked to him, and then we had lunch in Ebagoola.

Ted was the only inhabitant and he lived in a little tin and bark shanty at the bottom of the street near the creek. He had lived there alone ever since the place finally folded up. He talked volubly and Corporal Otto showed him some splicing and plaiting tricks with rawhide. We heard how a namesake of one of us, a prospector, disappeared in the ranges forever with only his horse returning 'a good while ago'. Old Ted said he had a photograph of John, the prospector's son, in his humpy. Visions of tracing our eccentric bachelor Uncle Sam, who disappeared into the North and had come back just once in sixty-three years, came to mind. The story of the son John, and the possibility of an unacknowledged wife and family, were intriguing. We went with Ted to his rubbish-packed house. He rummaged in the dark interior and produced a stiff-backed photograph of a strong, black-bearded gentleman dressed in a style of long ago.

'The father who perished?' we asked.

'No, the son, and a fine lad he was, too. Broke his neck when his horse stumbled and threw him,' Old Ted said.

'Well,' we said, puzzled, 'how long ago did the *father* die?'

'In the Palmer Rush days,' Ted said, '– in 1874.'

On the back of the picture he had written, 'I found this photograph.'

Ted was seventy-four, and he walked with a slight limp. He praised us as superior to the usual 'cut of the younger generation' because we ran after his hat when it blew off his old white head. Nailed to his belt he wore a curious block of wood.

'An invention of my own,' he told us. It was part of a truss for his hernia. Inside this, for added leverage, he had an empty

Ted was the only inhabitant and he lived in a tin and bark shanty.

metal matchbox. On the rump side, beneath his belt, he had another slab of tin to give further pressure. He hobbled along philosophically, his battered boots tied, and retied, with green-hide till they looked like dilapidated sandals. He said his hernia used to 'slip out', causing him sciatica, until he perfected his invention.

We presented Old Ted with a few tins of bully beef and a pound of tea which he acknowledged with a gleeful cackle. Although tea was rationed then, and hard to get, he seemed to value the cans more than the contents – 'to remember you by', he said. He said he was a great one for keeping things to remember people by. It was then that we understood his crazy hut full of bits of strap-leather, bundles of feathers, literally hundreds of empty tins and bottles, screws, rusty stirrup-irons and things. Each of these scraps had its association for Old Ted – of some person or place or experience which he could recall whenever he looked at them. In old Ebagoola Ted was alone day after day, month after month, with only the weekly mailman to speak to. Those bits of paper and rusty fragments of iron were his friends.

84

Then we walked through the old town – through the partly demolished dance hall where there are dozens of pairs of rusted roller skates, and an old piano that was falling to pieces as the termites bit tunnels in its vitals. On the walls were framed prints, conventional of the eighties. Termites were in these too. There was a full-size billiard table, with its green felt ripped and faded, and its legs eroded by insects. There were battered metal lamps, rust-spoiled rifles and verdigrised unspent cartridges.

In the butcher's shop the twin blocks were still sitting in the place where the town butcher used them. Then we went into the corner pub – the last standing of the several dozen shanties that sold grog in the boom days of the last century. In the pub, as in the other buildings, were piles of account books and business correspondence, diaries and bills, and letters with old colonial stamps that would make the eyes of a philatelist glisten. The last inhabitants had seemingly left Ebagoola with little more than they could carry. Behind them they left a record of their hopes and struggles, their disappointments and final defeat, for anybody who cared to see.

Andy who kept the pub was a fair example. His writings dated from the early years of this century until near the time when the exodus took place. Andy lived a not very comfortable, though not unhappy, life with his wife Bessie. He sold grog, and dealt in horses and cattle as a sideline. A glance at his books showed that in a typical year his profits were only £278 – a little over five pounds a week for the most important business in the community. He had many bad debts – £100 that year – and he often lost money by extraordinary evil turns of chance. Some years his horses died, or were unsaleable for cash after long overland trips made especially to dispose of them. And there was a disastrous quartz-crushing venture. Bulky books of blank script lay loose in the chaos of rubbish.

The papers revealed many other things. In the Depression years Andy had to stave off borrowing relatives down south who obviously thought their publican relative on the Peninsula as wealthy as Carnegie. There were letters from Andy's creditor friends who reminded him of money he owed them. He tried to pay them back, with indifferent success. He was urged by friends to send Bessie away for a rest because she had a 'bad heart'. But Andy could not afford to do this, or perhaps Bessie did not want to go.

A faded diary notes the course of one northern summer, when

the sun burned the tin roofs and parched the hills around the settlement.

'December 27th. Came home [from coast]. Bessie well.

'December 28th. Bessie took a bad turn about 9 a.m. and bad all day.

'10 p.m. improving. Just started raining.'

So the tropical monsoon for that summer began. Soon it would pour incessantly. For months it would flood the rivers, sweeping a mighty muddy torrent into the Gulf. Sixty thousand head of cattle were swept to sea in one 'wet'.

Then, on January 8th. 'Married 45 years today. Married in 1869 on 8th January.' Then, '27th March, 77 years of age. Mending gear today.'

Much advice came from Andy's sister Maud who lived in a suburb of Brisbane and believed in God. She wrote constantly urging the old couple to 'give themselves to God' and to pay back the £50 she lent them and to 'render themselves a living sacrifice acceptable to Him'.

But she lent Andy another £10.

Two years later came wires and letters of condolence, for the patient Bessie, after many more 'bad turns', had died. Old Andy now suffers with a 'bad leg'.

'November 5th. Mail Day. My foot is improving.

'November 6th. Mail Day yesterday. My foot is worse.'

A couple more years trailed disconsolately past. Then the correspondence and diary ceased abruptly. Andy was dead.

We took some of the papers of Ebagoola away with us to read around remote campfires as we got farther into the wilderness. Soon we were able to clear the name of one of Ebagoola's most respected citizens, the Chinese Ah Fong, from the aspersions of Sergeant Beach. Merely on the strength of a hasty glance at a few ledger entries the Sergeant alleged that Ah Fong was a notorious drunkard, forever on the 'turps'.

It was not so. Ah Fong's hotel account for November, 1910, for example, amounted to only £3.6.0, a ridiculously small figure when the heat, the wet, the boredom and the customs of the country are considered. We found also (from our researches into the papers from the butcher's and grocer's establishments) that Ah Fong lived almost exclusively on corn beef and flour, plus an occasional piece of fresh steak at sixpence per pound. Certainly he was no habitual drunkard as the Sergeant liked to make out; but on the evidence of Old Ted he was syphilitic. He was a fine citizen who 'helped to keep the Peninsula together'. He died, 'troubled with the syphilis', Ted said, not long before they deserted Ebagoola.

A few miles beyond the town we passed the grave plots where hundreds of the pioneers were buried. Their graves were surrounded by rough wire-netting, rusted through. Some were planted with garden flowers, half smothered by rank grass. One or two had a glass wreath-case. Some were bordered by corals and clam-shells carried one hundred miles over sea and plain and mountain from the Great Barrier Reef which twists down the north-east Australian coast. There were women's and babies' graves among them. The white-washed crosses were knocked down and rotten.

Today Ebagoola is scarcely even a ghost town because, since our visit, the blokes from the neighbouring settlement of Coen descended on its iron and timber, trucked them away and left little more than a few scars in the ground to tell its tale.

9

Cossack, on the other hand, is made of sterner stuff. It would need an expert demolition squad to level some of its massive walls. Those old convict craftsmen built well.

It would be good if the Western Australian Government appointed a local authority and granted him sufficient funds to have the place kept in repair. That the buildings were convict made is the more, not less, reason for their preservation.

The majority of the convicts were not bad blokes. This traditional Australian view has sometimes come under fire directed by noisy little chaps of a local geographical race of Angry Young Men. Some of the reluctant early arrivals were undoubtedly 'most notorious offenders, every one . . . as great a villain as ever graced a gibbet' but these were relatively few. There is a simple explanation for this. Under the English law of the day a man could be hanged for stealing an article of a value more than one shilling, and so most of the grievous sinners were not, unless possessed of rich or 'noble' connections, given the choice of migration. A surprising number of gentlemen were convicted for availing themselves of goods worth tenpence. By fixing the value at this, at first sight enigmatic, sum the Establishment of the day got rid of the chap and at the same time invested itself with a warm glow of humanitarianism by letting him remain alive. Some convicts were politcal or industrial exiles, like the Tolpuddle Martyrs of 1833, and others were superior men 'never known to associate with the common herd'. These, too, were comparatively few in number. Most of the people despatched to Botany Bay were sent after summary judgements carried out upon their conviction for petty pinching in the towns, or poaching in the countryside.

The briefest glance at official records will fill any normal person with compassion for many who were transported, and a contempt for the system that despatched them. Thus, William, the tailor's boy who was sentenced for life on May 31st, 1827, for stealing a handkerchief, his first offence. Mary Anne, who was eighteen, set fire to a haystack and was sentenced to twenty years. And John, a 'rough carpenter' twenty-one years old, was convicted on February 15th, 1827, for 'privately skating'. He was caught trespassing on a private pond in Bread Street, Cheapside. It was his first offence but the rough carpenter went out for life. Some such victims were children only thirteen years old when they were put into the hulks to await transportation.

If most of these people were ordinarily decent, and reasonably (by today's commercial and industrial standards) honest when they were sentenced, it is nevertheless true that many became soured, and some hopelessly embittered, by their treatment on the transports and after they landed. Anne, an assigned servant who spoilt a loaf of bread while baking, was given a sentence of seven days on bread and water. An exasperated convict who struck an officer was flayed with seventy-five lashes. A man who refused to lash his mate was himself given fifty lashes in punishment.

If the number of books stolen annually from the Radder by Oxford undergraduates, and the quantity of equipment removed from offices and factories by employees is any indication, it is probable that there is today scarcely a citizen of Australia or Britain who would not be a tolerably certain candidate for transportation as judged by late Georgian standards. Of the chaps who arrived in transports, many were of a scarcely less acceptable character, and of a rather more desirable heredity, than the reigning monarch of their day.

Roebourne then, inhabited and dreary; Cossack, deserted and full of charm; Port Sampson next and nearby, a quite horrifying little modern settlement of prefabricated bungalows built on the sand dunes. We left this place at speed. The desert highway now took us to Whim Creek. We could see the whim, but not the

Women accompanied the men.

Creek, though perhaps, during the rains, something like a stream ran somewhere nearby. Whim Creek has a population of two. Jack and his wife keep a rather mad-looking pub there. Reflectively, we each drank three schooners as the sun sank, and then drove in the rising moonlight to a creek fourteen miles out where we camped.

We paused at Port Hedland, gathering vital information about the activities of Whispering Smith, the good Father O'Dooley and other notable citizens. Here, as in all these old towns, the streets are as wide as The Mall, a provision, we were told, to allow the camel or bullock teams to turn round in the older days. After a mild session, we headed for the De Grey, a river on the edge of the once notorious Pardoo Sands. The De Grey was the goal of Warburton. This intrepid Englishman and some others started nearly ninety years ago from Alice Springs, in Central Australia, to cross the great deserts to the Western Australian coast. Theirs was a terrible journey. At length they reached the Oakover, a tributary of the De Grey, starving, exhausted, and almost naked.

Now, at last, they had plenty of water. They saw fish in the clear river. They deprived themselves of the entrails of birds for use as a bait, but the fish would not bite. On Christmas Day they drew a mental picture of their Adelaide friends at dinner whilst they 'should . . . be thankful to have the pickings out of any pig's trough'.

90

They were obsessed by the fear that when they got to the De Grey there might be no station there ('these far-off stations are sometimes abandoned'). But the station was still there, and from it came relief by men and horses. On these horses they covered the final 170 miles to the west coast, past the site of our present comfortable camp. Warburton had started with seventeen camels and ended with two. One died of poisoning, four ran away, three were left exhausted in the desert and seven were killed for food. Warburton reported that he had lost the sight of one eye and that his son was 'much shaken in health'. Sahleh the Afghan left his finger in Roebourne, but beyond this Warburton knew of no harm that had been done. In conclusion, he acknowledged the goodness and mercy of Almighty God, and expressed his gratitude to the whole colony of Western Australia.

The De Grey was dry. It is about 600 yards wide where we crossed on a barren expanse of sand speckled with stranded logs and smaller driftwood knotted against the odd trees that grow in its bed. These were a reminder of the mighty torrents that periodically sweep out of the inland during the rains. We talked with a party of aborigines camped in the river bed. They had quit their station jobs, as they are prone to do, and had gone on a hunting walkabout and a 'pink-eye'. This is aboriginal slang for holiday, derived from their condition at the end of it. Some were done up in hunting regalia, and all seemed carefree and happy. Several women accompanied the men. After their pink-eye, they said, they would return to work. Here, too, we heard a glorious sky song, and after a great deal of eye-strain we found its author, the bushlark *Mirafra javanica*, a trembling speck, higher than any skylark at heaven's gate.

We saw a blue-winged kookaburra, the tropical one that does not laugh. To a south-eastern Australian, a kookaburra that doesn't laugh is a bit of a fraud, for, from the earliest colonial days, the so-called bushman's clock has held a strong place in the affections of our people. The laugh of the kookaburra was commented on by all the early writers, pleasantly or otherwise according to their own character and circumstances. The gloomy novelist Marcus Clarke, spoke of 'horrible peals of semi-human laughter', but Grant and Ensign Barallier of the *Lady Nelson* spoke of the 'Laughing Bird . . . whose note can only be compared to the ha! ha! of a hearty laughing companion'.

That night the moon was full, a great golden orange ball that

Head of Iatra
R— Dyzen G.

After their pink-eye, they said, they would return to work.

rose through the drooping leaf-blades of the cabbage gums. To-morrow would be a good hard day for we would assail the Pardoo Sands, a flat stretch of nastiness fronted by the Eighty Mile Beach and backed by the 'hills of drifting sand, the barren plains and the ominous red haze of the desert' that deterred Gregory when he discovered the De Grey almost exactly one hundred years ago. For professional reasons, too, we were interested in tomorrow's journey. The dry, wide, almost treeless expanse that we had to cross is a faunal barrier that keeps much of the tropical life from penetrating farther down the coast towards south-western Australia.

The Pardoo Sands was one of the toughest leads in the west of former days. The Sands are lightly covered by semi-desert plants on which stock can exist – but it takes a million acres to carry a mere twenty thousand sheep. Yet the Sands caused us no trouble. Their teeth had been drawn by a recent grading and top dressing of the road, and in very few places did the vehicle show the least hesitation in getting through. On the same afternoon we made the better country of Anna Plains on the other side.

This is the first of the cattle properties and the owner was kind enough to sell us petrol and to produce a bottle of Scotch. His young wife from South Kensington, S.W.7, told us that she liked the life on the remote station. Nearby we saw our first northern bird, a glorious red-winged parrot that had been allowed this far south by a tongue of timber that speared into the yellow of the grass-lands. We saw more emus than before, which pleased us, and some plain turkeys – bustards – which pleased us even more. We did not molest them. Then we saw brolgas – native companions – in flock. The brolga is a big crane, the only true crane in Australia. It stands between three and four feet high and its wings span seven feet when it soars. Its general colour is silvery grey, but it has yellow eyes, and a head of red and olive-green. The old bushmen say that native companions dance the quadrille in company by moonlight. Certainly they display in small groups most charmingly, the silver of body and red of head moving prettily against the green of the reedy swamps to which they come to feed and drink.

The great wings of the brolga sometimes take it high over the Pardoo Sands and as far south as Onslow, but it is characteristically a bird of the north. Another beautiful tropical bird that we now saw on the trip for the first time was the curiously cavorting spangled drongo. This species is a pioneer, the sole representative in Australia of a family that spreads right across from Africa to Japan.

In Australian slang a drongo is a bit of a galah, a goat or a no-hoper. Zoologists often wonder why the names of a big pink-and-grey cockatoo, and the vivacious glossy drongo, should be used as terms of opprobrium.

In regard to *Dicrurus bracteatus*, Melbournians perhaps have the answer. Drongo was the name given to a horse that raced on Melbourne tracks from 1924 to 1926. Drongo was a good galloper, but it is said that he was never quite able to win on big occasions; he was, in short, second rate. So the language was enriched. Any gentleman who arouses the contemptuous disapprobation of an Australian is apt to be described as a bloody drongo.[1]

[1] Our friend Dato Loke Wan Tho has given us a clue to the possible origin of the slang usage of 'galah'. In Malaya *gila* (pron. gee-la) means 'mad'; hence *orang gila*, a madman. On the other hand, the modern expression may derive from the old bush saying 'As mad as a treeful of galahs'.

And so we came to Broome, the pearlers' town, the gateway to the rich grounds of the Timor Sea. Before we got there we ran out of the pindan scrub into the flat and featureless Roebuck Plains. The *Roebuck* was Dampier's ship on his second and legitimate voyage. Dampier's Australian story began when he was a member of the crew, probably the supercargo, of the buccaneering vessel *Signet*. This vessel has been generally called the *Cygnet* but that spelling is said to have been playfully adopted by the buccaneers because the captain's name was Swan. When the *Signet*'s crew mutinied and marooned the skipper, Dampier stayed with the ship. After a time the *Signet* needed an overhaul, and the buccaneers sailed for the largely unexplored western coast of New Holland, by now known to navigators from the fragmentary accounts of Dutchmen who had made accidental landfall here. In January, 1688, the *Signet* was anchored and careened in what is now called Cygnet Bay, in King Sound. There was friction between Dampier and his shipmates. After one disagreement concerning their final destination, he was 'threatened to be turned ashore on New Holland for it, which made me desist, intending, by God's blessing, to make my escape the first place I came neare'.

The *Signet* left the Broome area after a stay of a little more than three months. Dampier reached England after deserting the pirates in Nicobar. There he wrote his *New Voyage Round the World* which aroused enough interest among savants for them to recommend His Majesty William III to commission the author to make another exploratory voyage to New Holland.

Now Dampier was in the relatively well-found *Roebuck*. He made landfall in 1699. He explored and named Sharks Bay but was unable to find fresh water. So he went north to the Dampier Archipelago, near where we were now, and later home to London. Dampier made many observations on the bird fauna, but this was before men had found the means of preserving bird skins. He did, however, press some plants that found their way into the Herbarium at Oxford and seventeen Australian specimens are there still.

On neither voyage did Dampier think much of the country nor its dark inhabitants. Perhaps he compared the Kimberley *pindan* – scrubby, low savannah – with the green of his native Somerset. In any case, after the lush and teeming isles of the Indies, this flat and apparently barren coast must have been depressing. Its inhabitants, he decided, were 'the miserablest people in the world'.

Successive editions of Dampier's works resulted in bibliographical complexities that are of much interest to modern students of Australiana but, among contemporary scholars, it was perhaps only upon Jonathan Swift that their impact resulted in anything of lasting significance. It is almost certain that it was from Dampier's voyage to Sharks Bay that the proud and tragic Dean of St Patrick's took his location of the 'country of the Houyhnhms'. Swift's map was taken from Dampier's; and his Lemuel Gulliver, surgeon and sea-captain, was made out to be a cousin of the author of A Voyage to New Holland, Etc., in the year 1699.

It was a century or so before any navigator had anything good to say about this part of Australia. Lort Stokes went ashore in 1838 after rain and was shocked to find that 'everything wore a green and most delightful appearance'. Stokes believed that an immense bushfire had preceded the rainfall. 'The rain descends once more upon a dry and thirsty soil, and, from that very hour which seemed the date of cureless ruin, nature puts forth her wondrous power with increased effort, and again her green and flower-embroidered mantle decks the earth with a new beauty.'

10

Our first sight of Broome across the plain had something of the quality of a mirage. The white painted, iron buildings seemed to float in the air just above the horizon. As we got closer they certainly lost their ethereal look. Those of us who already knew Broome were looking forward to savouring it again. Those who did not were even keener. There is no other place like Broome in Australia. It has an Asian flavour. Yet one feels that it could be in no other country for it is completely bush Australian in its manners and outlook.

We drove along the foreshore and saw a large steam ship lying squat in the mud alongside the jetty. The sea had gone, yet the ship remained. Aboard, the chaps worked on unconcernedly with their unloading. On this north-western coast the tides rise more than thirty feet. Ships come in at high-water and tie up. By next morning the water has retreated farther than you can see. When the tide changes, the water comes in again and covers the mud-flats with a dangerous rush.

There was no jetty in the eighties, when Broome was the chief port of entry to the Kimberley gold rush. They had to man-handle every ounce of equipment through the deep mud from ship to beach. The naturalist Saville Kent visited 'the port of

96

At dances everybody performs with enormous verve.

Broome in Roebuck Bay' in the next decade. Landing, he said, was a gruesome undertaking for most. And even for a born naturalist, the half a mile of mud and its contents, 'a spotted whelk here, and there a winkle all new to him if not to science became a somewhat toilsome pleasure'. On leaving Broome, Saville Kent had to wade out once more, this time encumbered with a black cockatoo at wrist, a cage of live lizards under arm, and boots slung at neck. 'A clean-swept landing stage is the devoutly-to-be-wished-for innovation looked forward to by the writer on the occasion of his next visit to Roebuck Bay.' Nevertheless, he said, Broome was even then in direct touch with 'the hub of the world' by cable station.

There are three pubs in Broome. The Roebuck is the pearlers' pub. It was here that, up till a few years ago, ladies were publicly auctioned by mutual consent of vendor and the item of sale. It is a matter of general regret that ease of modern communications – aircraft and strangers arriving several times a week – is tending to break down the immoral fibre of Broome and to drive such occasional auctions underground. Further, we understand, improved communications have lowered prices alarmingly. It was recently calculated that the price per pound weight of the last lady sold was rather less than the selling price of prime beef on the hoof.

We stayed one night at the Continental Hotel, locally called 'The Conti'. This is the fashionable pub. Here carefully dressed business chaps stay during their brief visits by air. Here, too, are the remains of an open-air theatre where live shows used to take place many years ago. Nowadays The Conti holds a dance once a week, as do the other two pubs on different nights. The orchestra at The Conti is composed of Ah Chee, the local Chinese garage-keeper, who plays fast jazz on the sort of piano that Miss Winifred Atwell would admire. He is accompanied by a Malay who plays the tea-box. This is an uncomplicated instrument composed of a lidded tea-chest and a broom handle. The broom handle is tied to the side of the tea-chest with a string. When the broom handle is placed upright on the lid of the tea-chest the taut string makes a double bass of perhaps surprising effect. At the dances everybody – Japanese, Malays, whites and hybrids – performs with enormous verve. There is, of course, a certain degree of class consciousness in that whites and non-whites tend to partner their own kind. But everybody is on the floor together and there is a good deal of mixed dancing.

Apart from schoolgirls' basketball there is in Broome no organized sport, or any such nonsense. The three pubs are the principal meeting places of townspeople and pearlers alike. Drinking begins at breakfast time and from then on the drinking population moves from pub to pub until closing time at 11 p.m. To the casual visitor, the most extraordinary thing of all is the apparent lack of drunkenness.

The third pub is the Governor Broome – the 'G.B.' The proprietress is Mrs Eunice South, a woman of enormous charm and energy. She runs not only the hotel but has reared a fascinating menagerie of pet birds and other animals. The birds are mostly quarrions and cockatoos. The G.B. clientele have taught the corellas to swear in a quite splendid manner. Their unexpectedly rich, wild north-western vocabulary disconcerts tourists ashore from visiting ships. Mrs South cheerfully accepts this position and delights in the confusion of any toffee-nosed visitor from 'The South'.

In Broome nobody walks anywhere. The taxis are communal, and all fares cost two shillings whether you want to go a hundred yards or so to the next pub, or three miles to a lugger at the edge of the town. At any time a taxi may contain several people of different colours going to various places. Anybody with two shillings is entitled to whistle a taxi whether it is empty or not.

Mrs South's parrots spend much of their time whistling the taxis which are continually discharging and picking up G.B. clientele. For some time it was matter of serious debate why the corellas always whistled to taxis and ignored private cars. For a while many attributed an almost human intelligence to her lusty birds. Then the explanation was found. All taxis in Broome are modern Holdens, an American-designed Australian car. The engine of the Holden has a characteristic low purr. Over the years the corellas have come to associate the special purr of the Holden (and not the noises of other makes) with shrill whistles from the pub's verandah. So it is that whenever they hear a Holden, the cockatoos, too, faithfully whistle and the drivers back up their vehicles, unsure whether or not there is another two bob in the offing.

We liked the atmosphere of the G.B. best, and asked Mrs South could we stay there when we had a few days' leisure on our way back south.[1] Then we took to the road. We wondered where was the party that had crossed the continent from the east, which we expected to meet within the next hundred miles and a day or so. We left town at 7.30 that night and camped out beyond the Broome-Derby road junction. The following afternoon we pulled in under the boabs and the white-barked gums on to the bank of the West Hardman and made our camp. The baobab or bottle tree is a common, and bizarre, sight throughout the north-west. Saville Kent found it 'most extravagantly droll'. Except when very young, each baobab is an individual like no other. Baobabs grow in all shapes from 'smooth symmetrically-shaped radishes' to 'rough-rinded mangold-wurzels of Brobding-nagrian proportions'.

The explorer Grey described a baobab as a 'gouty-stemmed tree', and imagined that it might be diseased. Later he was to see hundreds 'affected in the same way' and realized that there was nothing pathological about their grotesque anatomy. The swollen stern is an adaptation toward fluid storage in dry regions. The swollen trunk of the bottle tree has been likened to the camel's hump; a comparison would be rather more valid if the camel did, in fact, store water in its hump. The substance of the boab tree yields not only fluid but a white edible gum which is said to make a good drink when dissolved in hot water.

[1] It is sad to relate that the G.B. is now some sort of a hostel; it is a pub no more. Alas, nothing these days is sacred.

The 'gouty stemmed' baobab, a 'most extravagantly droll' tree.

We built our fires and soon had cooking a splendid meal of galah. Most people will not believe that the galah cockatoo makes good food. Although about one third of the population of Australia live near cities, the bush and its traditions are always very close and almost everybody is a reasonably efficient camper and a self-confessed authority on bush cookery. But Pitt and Collins Street bushmen will never believe that the big pink cockatoo makes good meat. The fact is that the meat of tolerably young galahs is little, if at all, inferior to that of pigeons. This great truth is not new. As early as 1801 Grant of the *Lady Nelson* said: 'Nor is the flesh of the parrot disagreeable, having very much the same taste as our pigeon.' Most people, of course, have never eaten parrot; nor (in Australia) pigeon either, for that matter.

So the old recipe for galah persists as follows:

Take one galah, prepare it carefully, and cook with one piece of quartz over a slow fire. When the rock is soft, the galah is fit to be eaten.

A variation of the old bush joke is:

When the quartz is soft, throw the galah away.

When we had time, we simmered our birds in a shallow pan for about half an hour. Often we curried them, with delicious results. Ivan, the kangaroo shooter, was engaged in this rewarding pastime when the other party found us under the white gums and the baobabs. We were well pleased. Soon there was a rush for pannikins, for Dom had let the moths out of his pocket at Broome and was brandishing a bottle of Scotch.

I I

We broke camp early on the following morning and together we all set out for the Fitzroy Crossing where we wanted to refuel and stock up with stores at Dick Fallon's pub, and meet an American zoologist, Donald Farner, who was flying up from Perth to join the party.

We were now a convoy of three vehicles. There were the big Land Rover, Serventy's small one (pulling its trailer) and Ivan's heavy duty Dodge utility on which he could carry at least a ton of gear. All the vehicles were fitted with long-range petrol and water-tanks so that we could at any time set up camp in remote regions that lacked surface water.

Dick Fallon welcomed us at the pub, and everyone dived for the showers and cleaned off the dust. We broke out some clean clothes from our swags, and then foregathered about Dick's new bar where he shouted the lot of us cold beer. That night we had dinner at the pub.

Suddenly we heard a burst of something like rifle fire out near the bar. Of course it could not have been rifle fire – obviously some one was playing the fool with Chinese crackers – and so we went on with our steak and eggs. But when we went across the quadrangle a little later to have a few jugs before turning in, Dick was in a mildly indignant mood.

'I don't mind a bit of fun,' he said, 'but when the boys start chucking lead about it's another matter.'

It was Paddy, the carpenter, who had caused the pother. In this tropical land the bar has a good strong roof but there is only one wall and from this the counter juts as an oblong shaded promontory. For no reason that anybody could discover, Paddy had retired to the nearby sleeping quarters. From the verandah he had amiably started shooting bottles and glasses off the counter. The chaps did not like this very much. They stiffened themselves against the one protective wall and waited.

'There were bullets and glass all over the place,' said Old Dick, 'and just then Harmonious Harry walked in – and a couple of bullets went past his ear like bees. And Harmonious Harry took umbrage – and I don't blame him either.'

As far as we could discover, this was the one thing that had irritated Harmonious Harry in the past thirty years.

The mildly antisocial behaviour of Paddy, and the bland but firm police action that almost immediately followed, set us thinking about some of the differences, as well as the convergent similarities, between the Australian 'never-never' and the American 'West' in the pioneering days. Although much of outback Australia and the United States were settled at the same time, there were never allowed to arise in Australia those odious phenomena, the 'gun-slinger' and the 'bounty-hunter', currently idealized on North American television. We believe this dissimilarity to be almost certainly bound up with the systems of justice under which the respective countries developed. In North America, they generally elected their sheriffs, marshals and judges, and grew tolerant of the incompetence and corruption inevitable in functionaries who depend on the popular vote for their livelihood. In Australia the British system of government appointments prevailed and, whenever a new settlement began, there moved in a unit of the official police force. Lawless men there were in plenty in the Australian colonial days, but these were never allowed to stalk through towns with guns in their belts. If they persisted in their malefactions they had to hide in the hills. They became *bush-rangers* who, when in need of funds or horses, *stuck-up* or *bailed-up*, stage-coaches, sheep stations and, occasionally, banks. If one of these men singly showed his face in a township he would be promptly put in gaol by the local police. Billy the Kid could never have arisen in Australia. At the outset of his career he would have had his bottom kicked, and his little pistol taken away from him. Likewise, that loathsome phenomenon, the bounty-hunter, was never spawned in Australia where it was held that, given the establishment of a proper police force, it was their job, except in very unusual circumstance, to bring bad men to justice. The acceptance of blood-money was held to be an outrage to bush morality. In Australia a bounty-hunter would have found nobody to drink with.

We met Donald Farner at the nearby airstrip, loaded up the trucks and set out in convoy for Fossil Downs, only seventeen miles away.

Most of us had met Farner previously in Europe or in the United States and we were glad to have him with us. A chunky, humorous graduate of Wisconsin, Don went well in the bush and with the curious people we encountered on the track. Even Ivan Carnaby (who dislikes graduates, Yanks, bot-flies, snakes and Eastern Staters) thought Farner a fairly good type.

Nevertheless, Farner had one trick that at once set him apart from the rest of us. He seemed to be addicted to pills. Later we discovered that he was neither hypochondriacal nor a drug addict – he was simply taking no chances with his health. We insisted that there is in Australia no risk of dysentery or other such enteric abomination, but Farner had travelled too much in Europe to take unnecessary chances. He reminisced gloomily about the Latin countries, of British Railways and the English veal and ham pie. Every time he had a drink from one of the canvas bags he carefully doctored the water.

We crossed the Fitzroy and then headed for the Margaret River a few miles above the junction of the two dry river beds. We crossed the Margaret at another new causeway and turned along the north bank towards the Fossil Downs homestead which lies a couple of miles farther on.

Fossil Downs is the home of Bill and Maxine MacDonald, and their two daughters. The station is about the size of a largish English county, say a little bigger than Essex, Kent or Cumberland. The homestead is an oasis of green lawns, good books, cool beer and nice people in a jumble of low limestone ranges that were once part of the flat sea floor. The upflung ridges are studded with the shells of sea creatures that crawled in Upper Devonian times, perhaps 270 million years ago. Visitors who lack the time or energy to pick up fossils for themselves can see trilobites embedded in the verandah flagstones. In an embrasure within the homestead staircase is a shaggy canvas water-bag, a relic that goes strangely well in its modern surroundings. Fossil Downs was the end-point of one of the longest cattle treks in Australian history. The brothers MacDonald left Goulburn, near Sydney, in March 1883 with fifty horses, seven hundred head of cattle and high hopes. They crossed the Blue Mountains and set out on an enormous semi-circular lead of 3,500 miles. Those who finished the journey reached the Kimberleys in July 1886, after a not unremarkable journey through forest and desert, and often hostile aborigines, to settle and prosper near the clear and permanent waters of the Fitzroy.

We asked Bill about Geikie Gorge. He told us we were welcome to go there, camp, and collect. He drew us a professional map of the route to the entrance of the gorge, and offered us the use of his ten-foot fibre-glass dinghy and outboard motor. With this we could travel the length of the gorge, landing almost wherever we chose. We could not have hoped for anything better.

The entrance to the gorge is just above the confluence of the Fitzroy and the Margaret. We were told that to get there meant travelling over wide stretches of heavy sand, so we decided to leave Ivan's truck at Fossil Downs and to take only the vehicles with four-wheel drive. The dinghy was lashed on its own trailer behind Dom's vehicle and his own trailer left behind. We set off in the late afternoon. We followed the rough and narrow track in and out of the dry river beds, and groaned across the sandy reaches in low ratio until we rounded the point near the entrance to the gorge.

It was a startling blue in the afternoon sunlight. This great sheet of water extends for miles, with tropical green foliage surmounted by towers of limestone that take on a pinky glow. It was magnificent. We ran the trucks up through an opening in the scrub on to the steep bank. Not without some trouble though, for the big vehicle began to sand-bog and we had to hitch a tow-rope from the back of the small one. Then, with both trucks pulling in low ratio, we got the big fellow through. We set up camp in a grove of cajaputs that were in blossom, with a background of tall, broad-leaved Leichhardt trees. The still waters of the gorge came to the bank immediately below, and this made a convenient mooring for the dinghy which was soon unlashed and floated.

While we made camp Tim fitted the outboard and gave it a trial run. She ran well, and then some of us piled aboard like schoolboys on an outing and started off for a quick look down

Tim and Ivan counted more than a dozen crocodiles.

the gorge. The evening light was almost incredibly lovely. The stillness of the water carried the reflections of the trees. We went down to where the great limestone walls reared out of the water, perpendicularly above us. They were startlingly white at their bases, where the floodwaters of the rainy season had washed and cut them into grottoes and traceries. Above, the rains had weathered the rock into shapes that recalled Egyptian sculpture, with a curious fluting in the soft red stone. In parts, the high walls were a vivid red that ran into amber, all deeply etched with the sharp shadows of evening. This was a place of beauty and majesty, entirely unspoilt by Europeans and with luck, we thought, it might be kept so for centuries. Thankfully we headed back to camp with plans for a long river trip the following day.

Ivan was out shooting. We collected wood for the fire and boiled the billy. With unlimited water at our door-step, we did some much needed washing. We hung the wet clothes on bushes. Bill had advised us not to swim. The waters of the gorge, like all northern streams, abound with the small freshwater Johnston's crocodile, principally a fish-eater that does not attack man. These grow to only about five feet long. But there is always the chance that a big estuarine crocodile may, after the wet season, be locked up in any sizeable stretch of water like the Geikie. These brutes are sometimes twenty feet long and even the smaller examples are rough customers. They generally attack from the water.

Ashore, outside their traditional hunting element, they are thoroughly frightened of man. But in the water their innate and horribly successful trick is to move silently towards bank, or canoe, with little more than protuberant nostrils and eyes showing as slow moving islets above the surface. Then there is a sharp explosive rush out of the water with open jaws. The victim is seized, and a swift back-lash takes him below. Though securely held, a man may sometimes escape if he controls his fear and agony and has a lot of luck. For man, unlike the crocodile, can think; and if he remembers, and can find one of the reptile's eyes, a gouging finger-nail will often cause the creature to let go. Then perhaps the man will get away and, though torn and bleeding, may perhaps struggle ashore before the next attack.

That night Ivan and Tim took an electric torch and guns, and walked down along the water's edge to look for crocodiles. It was easy to pick up the ruby glitter of their eyes as they lay floating on the surface. The fiery red of the eye of the crocodile, like the green of the cat's, comes from the internal tapetum, a reflection device operating in the same principle as the 'cat's eyes' set in the surface of roads. It has evolved in a great variety of nocturnal animals, and it helps them to take advantage of every scrap of starlight in their darkened haunts.

Tim and Ivan counted more than a dozen small crocodiles and Ivan, more as a gesture than in the hope of bagging one, fired one barrel from his twelve bore at a particularly cheeky little brute near the water's edge. The blast blew it clean out of the water, but before the surprised Ivan could run forward to grab it by the tail, the crocodile twisted about and splashed back beneath the surface to deep water.

Professional crocodile shooting is usually done from the safety of boats. The trick is to keep a brilliant light fixed on the reptile while the boat drifts quietly up to it. If the hunter gets close enough he can destroy its brain with a single shot from a ·303 rifle. Quickly now, before it sinks, a harpooner drives a spear into the heavy body. The spear has a detachable head fixed to a rope. The big crocodile is then hauled alongside, or buoyed so that it can be picked up later. Ashore, the whole of the belly skin from throat to tail is cut away and dried. The value of the skin is estimated at so much an inch across the girth.

There was not much use setting a night line for the giant perch, the so-called barramundi, with so many small crocodiles about. There would not be much left of a fish when we hauled it in next morning. Luckily, we were not in need of rations, for Maxine MacDonald had loaded us up with beef and, miraculously, a large box of fresh vegetables. After we had fed ourselves, Ivan soon had the beef simmering in a camp oven for the next day's tucker and we were contented enough.

As soon as darkness fell we had become aware of the flying foxes. These are large fruit-bats. Their sharp features somewhat resemble those of a fox. The flying foxes flapped above us among the cajaputs, feeding on the heavily scented blossoms, and quarrelling and squealing shrilly. We turned torches on them and shot one for identification. It was about as big as a fair-sized cat. In the years gone by, the aborigines gathered in camps and feasted on these big bats.

At first sight, sound and smell, one could hardly think of a less attractive and more malodorous meal. This opinion seems to have been shared by the first white man known to have seen one in Australia. He was a sailor ashore from Cook's *Endeavour* while she was being careened in north Queensland after striking the Barrier Reef in 1770. The sailor claimed that he had seen the devil. 'He was,' says John, 'as large as a one gallon keg, and very like it; he had horns and wings, yet he crept so slowly through the grass that if I had not been *afeard*, I might have touched him.' The chronicler dryly recorded that this formidable apparition was afterwards discovered to have been a bat. 'They have indeed no horns but the fancy of a man who thought he saw the devil might easily supply that defect.'

If soaked overnight in red wine and cooked gently they make a fair enough meal, but we suppose that the same could be said of almost any fresh organic matter. In this camp we were too well found to bother with them. In any case Ivan, a conservative bushman, did not hold with eating flying foxes. Nor did Ivan hold with snakes, Dagoes, Pommies, Yanks nor people from 'The Eastern States'. Officers were particularly bad. That night we turned in to the accompaniment of Ivan's unsolicited views on army life and the evils thereof. An ageing militia officer called Lollylegs occupied a great part of the story.

It was at this camp that we got some understanding of an affair that had been bothering some of us for several years past.

Looking at Dom's face – a face benign in repose as he contemplatively swigged at a pannikin of rum and water in his swag near the fire – it was difficult to believe that here was one of the men most detested in the Pacific Theatre during the war against the Japanese. There was little about him now that would suggest that Dom was one of a group of persons whom many people wanted to indict as war criminals. Generally, if one is unfortunate enough to find oneself in the company of such a person, one tends to avoid like a plague the subject of former contention. But we had heard so many conflicting stories about the part that Dom had played in this unsavoury business that we felt that this would be a good opportunity to let him talk about it and, if he chose, to offer an explanation to us, an essentially sympathetic audience.

So in our tactful way we said suddenly, 'Tell us about your part in that rather disagreeable goldfish business during the war, Dom.'

There was silence, except for the crackling of the fire. Ivan, a close friend of Dom's, and once a soldier, stirred uneasily.

'It was not goldfish,' said Dom quietly. 'The fish is *Nematalosa erebi*, a so-called bony bream. It is, in fact, a true herring – one of the soft-rayed clupeoid fishes. It is a Perth fish, and therefore a good fish.'

There was another silence.

'It is true,' Dom started off again, 'that it does not command any sale when fresh. But is nevertheless a very fine fish, and it can be caught easily in great numbers by means of mesh nets of the beach seine type in the Swan River, the Leschenault Estuary and elsewhere. Leschenault was one of Peron's men in Baudin's expedition of 1801.'

'It would be rather pleasant if you didn't change the subject,' somebody said.

'Well,' resumed Dom, with some dignity, 'in World War II, Mr A. J. Fraser, Director of Fisheries, whom you have met, suggested to Mr Vincent Gardiner, whom you do not know, that as he was already engaged in the production of turtle soup, it might be extremely helpful to the war effort if he, Mr Gardiner, experimented with the canning of certain common Western Australian estuarine fishes, particularly Perth herring, for which there was no demand when fresh. It turned out to be a very good product,' concluded Dom, a little defiantly.

'But how did *you* get mixed up in these criminal activities?' somebody broke in.

'I was transferred home to Western Australia during the war to work on, among other things, the biology of the Perth herring

'It turned out to be a very fine fish. Not perhaps of the quality of good Scotch salmon, but nevertheless, a very good fish and, in tomato sauce, very similar to European herring.

'It is true, unfortunately, that the flesh is comparatively soft. Therefore it does not stand excessive handling during transport. When tins of Perth herring eventually reached the forward troops the fish was still tasty, but appearances were against it.

'Irrationally, the privates objected.

'Various personages associated with this delectable product, notably A. J. Fraser, Vincent Gardiner and myself went in some danger of our lives.

'It was even suggested that we be arraigned before the war criminal courts on charges of having conspired with the Japanese to lower morale.

'This charge is not true.'

There was silence except for the crackling of the campfire.

'It was an attractive product, I thought,' said Dom.

'I enjoyed them.

'It was an honest attempt urgently to step up production of a food in short supply.

'How were we to know they wouldn't travel?

'We did our best.

'*I would accept a tin of this fine Perth fish any time.*'

12

We were up at piccaninny light. After breakfast we loaded the dinghy with guns and cameras and sailed up the gorge. This must be one of the loveliest spots in Australia. The soft green of the cajaputs, one of the taller and more graceful of the melaleucas, contrasted with the brilliant, sun-dappled green of the water. It was a wonderful morning and we all felt that life was a pretty good affair. We floated around the bend where the limestone walls towered over us. We came to more groves of cajaputs wedged between red walls and water. Odd fruit-bats began to flap heavily out of the flowering trees. Then we saw them hanging in thousands from the branches like heavy black fruit.

Tim angled the boat towards the trees. When we were still about thirty yards away the bats took fright in droves. The black malodorous creatures exploded from the timber until the sky was clouded by flapping wings. Their shrill cries, and their wings, filled the gorge with sound. As they passed close overhead we could see the delicate skeletal structure of their arms etched against the thin wing-membranes and the bright sky. In their profusion, and in these surroundings, they seemed to us like creatures of the past; we all had the ridiculous feeling that we had unaccountably stepped back into a landscape of remote age. We spent a long

We floated around the bend where the limestone walls towered over us.

time watching the big bats, and when some of them returned we saw them expertly fasten themselves upside down to the thin, swaying branches of the melaleucas.

Then we found ourselves floating along where the water came right to the limestone cliffs, lapping through rocky grottoes. We surprised a darter, whose snake-like neck appeared above water. Some people call them snake-birds. We followed him. He dived again, and made for the shelter of a water filled cave. He showed his annoyance when we floated the boat in after him. We watched his sleek steely plumage against the bright patches of sunlight reflected on to the white limestone.

This stone is hard and brittle, and gives a metallic ring when struck. In places the water had dissolved it into thin traceries that hang down like reredos screens, delicate and of great beauty. In one long reach, the cliffs ahead resembled gigantic figures, and in other parts the gorge widened and there were wide banks with tall and big-leaved Leichhardts that gave shady glades.

It was good to land at these cool places for the October sun was hot towards midday. Up in the red cliffs we could almost always hear the liquid song of a particular bird. We all wanted to identify the hidden singer; its song was so beautiful, and it was obviously wedded in some curious way to the old red cliff faces. The quality of the notes suggested that it was a *Colluricincla*, a relative of the grey thrush that sings around Sydney and Melbourne gardens in spring and, like the European robin, in autumn too. If thrush it was, it could not be grey. It had to be red, or, at least, warm chestnut. No bird that lived on those ruddy walls could be anything else.

The cliff-singer was a hard bird to collect. It was numerous enough; perhaps, in fact, one of the commonest of the local birds. A shadowy form, it darted up and down and around the cliff faces, rarely pausing for more than a moment or two between cliff and tree and sky. Two of us at length took one each; and it was richly rufous in colour. We identified it as *C. woodwoodi*, the 'brown-breasted shrike thrush'. 'Rock' or 'cliff' thrush is the name we must use in future.

At daybreak there was movement about the camp. Those of us who were aware of it took no notice for we thought it was Ivan, who was usually up and out at piccaninny daylight. But it was not Ivan. It was a large and pensive wild boar making an inspection of our camp. Ivan awakened and watched the boar finish his tour. He – the boar – then walked unconcernedly away down the path that led to the river bed. Ivan slipped quietly out of his swag. He picked up a twelve-bore and tracked the boar through the scrub. He saw the big fellow saunter slowly across the sand-spit towards the far bank. He raised his gun. At that moment the pig stopped. It turned round, and gazed thoughtfully at Ivan. This disconcerted Ivan. While returning the animal's stare Ivan remembered that the cartridges in his gun contained only light shot for the collection of birds. The pig, having inspected Ivan, turned about and resumed his leisurely parade across the sand, back towards where he lived. Ivan, now rather thoughtful himself, about-turned also, and retraced his steps to where we lived. When we awoke, Ivan told us of his meeting, speculating on what the behaviour of the tusker might have been had its backside been rudely peppered with bird-shot. The imagined spectacle of Ivan racing for a tree with an outraged boar in pursuit was a genial beginning to our day.

The laymen of the party found the more specialized zoological talk to be laced with expressions that could be adopted in the usual slang of camp talk. There is always the memory of Dom Serventy, watchmaker's glass screwed in his eye and forceps poised, dictating information for one of us to enter in his notebook, a description that might end, 'No ossification, sexually immature.' A wonderful phrase this, which came to be applied with bizarre effect on other occasions. There is one memory of Dominic in another camp crouched over a weighing balance wedged between the thick roots of a boab tree which gave shelter from the dusty wind, his attitude one of intense concentration as he carefully adjusted the scale. What gave the scene an oddly picturesque touch was the khaki sou'wester hat that he was wearing, a form of headgear that contrasted violently with a shade temperature of 110 degrees and a scorched and dusty landscape.

Sartorially, we were not the sort of mob that Savile Row would approve. Most of us wore shorts, or khaki strides, and suede desert boots. Ivan, however, preferred his large elastic-sided boots. He kept his strides up with the wide belt, with a knife pouch attached, that is usually worn by bushmen. Personal taste in odd apparel was also reflected in the type of swags used.

The simplest was merely a voluminous sack into which one member thrust everything, from clothes to bedding. Things which he didn't need, or thought he didn't need, were stowed into a battered suitcase, borrowed in Perth, the catches of which soon ceased to function. Business letters and galley proofs were received from

Dom weighing bird specimens.   R.B.61

'No ossification, sexually immature.'

publishers at various out-of-the-way post-offices, air-mailed by a formidably efficient secretary in London. All these would be crammed into the suitcase. At various camps this wretched piece of luggage would manage, by some diabolic agency, to project itself from the opened door of the Land Rover and disgorge its confused contents in the dust. The owner would hurl himself on the mess with a roar like a scrub bull and wedge it back into the vehicle whence it would issue like a jack-in-the-box at the next camp. As more and more galley proofs arrived he stowed them about the vehicle amongst log books and maps, and would often proof-read them *en route,* or hand them to others to check through for printers' errors. Those galley proofs – the re-written 7th edition of Parker and Haswell's *Textbook of Zoology* – must surely have been the most travel-stained lot of paper that Macmillans have ever received.

Ivan had the largest swag. It consisted of an enormous amount of bedding. Besides blankets he even carried *sheets*, and a great mattress whose matted entrails bulged through its ruptured covering. All this he would roll into a tarpaulin of outsize proportions.

After years in the open Ivan believed in comfort at night. His swag, when laid out on an old Kalgoorlie stretcher, took on the aspect of a Victorian double bed. The incongruity of this extraordinary contrivance in the Kimberley landscape was not so much a cause of hilarity but rather, the inspiration of a feeling of awe. For those of us who slept meanly in a canvas swag upon the ground Ivan's great couch appeared like the bier of a potentate or the Great Bed of Ware.

On our last day in camp at Geikie Gorge we were visited by Merilee MacDonald who rode in from the distant homestead. Merilee was seventeen. She lunched with us as we ate the last of the excellent beef provided by one of her papa's best speyed cows expertly cooked by Ivan in the camp oven. It was very pleasant to have a guest as nice as Merilee, and we were absorbed in what she had to tell us of station life and the aborigines of her part of the country. Merilee grew up in the Kimberleys and had not long ago returned from boarding school in Perth. For a young girl she seems to be strangely in harmony with this ancient and beautiful land and has a deep sympathy for aborigines whom she has known from childhood and to whom she can talk in their own language.

We packed our gear and loaded the boat aboard the trailer. Merilee swung on to her horse and set out across country as we started across the wide stretches of sand of the dry river bed. We arrived back at Fossil Downs in the evening and drank beer with Bill and Maxine and told them what we had been doing. The MacDonalds put us up in the bunk house; sheer luxury, with hot showers and real beds. All this, and fresh clothes too, so inspired one of us to wear into the dinner the most rumpled Merton College tie that ever existed. This was a piece of one-upmanship on Dom Serventy, who was at that other place across in the swamps of Cambridgeshire, and who unaccountably had neglected to bring his tie with him. Serventy gazed at the other's tie in astonishment. Then he said that he now believed without question the story of the Balliol tie, the missionary and the cannibal chief. This was a hilarious evening. We cannot remember which of the two gentlemen was at Balliol.

Merilee took us to see a bower-bird's display-ground not far from the homestead. One of us set up a movie camera, but the bower builder refused to come back. It was here in the Kimberleys, on the Victoria River, in November 1839, that Captain John Lort Stokes 'found matter for conjecture in noticing a number of twigs

One of us set up a camera, but the bower-birds would not come.

with their ends stuck in the ground, which was strewed over with shells and their tops brought together so as to form a small bower'. Stokes first thought the structure to be 'some Australian mother's toy to amuse her child'. Then at Port Essington he was asked 'to go and see the "bird's playhouse" when I immediately recognized the same kind of construction I had seen at the Victoria River: the bird was amusing itself by flying backwards and forwards, taking a shell alternately from each side, and carrying it through the archway in its mouth'.

Today the display-ground of this lilac-crested grey bower-bird is apt to be strewn not only with shells, pebbles, bones, bits of precious opal and pieces of quartz but also with such objects as teaspoons, coins, fragments of broken glass, nails, beer-bottle tops and brass cartridge cases. In the Ord River country of the Kimberleys, an otherwise undistinguished gentleman named Edward Delaney acquired celebrity in the literature of zoology when his missing spectacles were found at the bower of a great grey bower-bird.

An Englishman, John Gould, probably coined the name 'bower-bird', and his description of the bowers and their decorations caught the imagination of the Victorian public. 'Bower-bird' became a household expression, generally applied to people, especially little girls, who collected odds and ends of colourful rubbish. The satin bower-bird of eastern Australia, a glossy blue-black beauty, was found to have a predilection for blue objects. This urge is so powerful that it often flies through the open windows of laundries to steal bags of washing blue. It will purloin delphiniums, petunias, hyacinths and other blue flowers almost from under the noses of gardeners. The spotted bower-bird, like the great grey, gathers principally pale or reflecting objects – bleached bones and shells, and latterly, broken glass, bits of tin, thimbles, screws, spoons, forks, coins and the like. It will hop through an open window on to a dressing table to steal jewellery. A spotted bower-bird once stole the ignition keys from a parked motor car. The aggrieved owner was shrewd enough to go to the nearest bower where he found them. Another bird stole the glass eye of a bushman from the table beside his bed.

The display-ground is the focal point of the male's interest. At it he displays violently, and to it his flashing movements and noise attract a potential mate. The male defends his bower territory and female savagely.

In several (but not all) bower-birds, the displaying male chooses and displays with objects coloured in the image of rival males. The male makes continuous threat gestures in display, but the threat is directed at the coloured ornaments, and not at the watching female who stands impassively within or behind the bower. She has all the appearance of unconcern or, if we may use an expression that smacks of anthropomorphism, boredom. Yet the excitable display of the male holds her interest. Its violence keeps rivals away. And so, if the male display is sufficiently attractive and aggressive, the female will still be at the bower when the mating time comes.

Once more we took to the road. We wanted to collect in the vicinity of Tunnel Creek and Winjana Gorge. We had a vague hope, too, that in the course of our assigned collecting duties, we might find a rare black grass-wren somewhere in the spinifex country beyond. This bird is known only from three unsexed skins taken about sixty years ago and it has not been heard of since. A rough track led us north towards the distant Oscar Range.

We hoped to get through the pass in the range before making evening camp. In this latitude darkness comes quickly for there is little twilight. Usually we made camp some time before sundown. This gave the collectors time to work before dark. The late afternoon and evening light is beautiful. It turns the whole land-scape to gold, and gradually the ranges glow red and purple in the slanting rays of the sinking sun. But now, as we drove over the rocky and dusty track the sun was still high in the sky, and the distance danced in the heat haze. Often we saw the twisting dust columns of willy-willies moving across the land. Sometimes they rolled in their wake the odd roly-poly, a prickly ball of dry vegetation, occasionally a yard in diameter.

A willy-willy is what is called a dust devil in many countries. It is a rotary vortex of air that appears suddenly when a gentle breeze is blowing across a blazing hot desert. A willy-willy can dump a man on to the ground; it can tear through a camp, and flatten and empty a row of tents without affecting others nearby; it can carry dust and other debris more than a thousand feet in the air. In parts of Western Australia they call them Cock-eyed Bobs.

You can get a bad buffeting and a car full of dust if you run into a big one careering wildly across country. Some years ago a man and his wife, who were making a tour by car of the Northern Territory, pulled up in the midday heat at an artesian bore. The promise of this cool, refreshing water was not to be denied. The lady got out of the dusty car, and in the middle

A rough track led us north towards the distant Oscar Range.

of the great deserted landscape, stripped off her clothes and stood under the overflow, savouring her first real bath for days. Then, scrubbed and clean, she started to walk towards the car for the towel proffered by her husband. Suddenly she found herself in the centre of a willy. It passed on rapidly, leaving her plastered from head to foot in a thin coating of bright red mud. The husband reported that it was an engaging sight.

Such vortices are essentially similar to the waterspouts that sometimes rise hundreds of feet above lakes and oceans. These are responsible for the frequently true reports of 'raining fishes'. From times at least as remote as A.D. 300 there have been descriptions of fishes falling with rain, usually after high winds. These fallen fishes are never more than a few inches long. They have been sucked up in a vortex, and sometimes carried miles from water before dropping with rain. There have also been reported falls of toads and turtles but these may not be authentic since these relatively heavy creatures sometimes emerge in hundreds from underground aestivation immediately heavy rain saturates their environment after a prolonged drought.

After winding miles through the spinifex we saw the tall shape of a windmill. Presently, through the light scrub, we came to the bore keeper's shed. The resident was an aboriginal employed by the station on whose run the bore was sunk. His job was to see that it kept working efficiently. He lived in this camp with two lubras and a variety of mongrel dogs. His only shelter was a bough shed which consisted quite simply of leafy branches laid over poles, open at the sides. A bough shed costs nothing and is easy to erect. Its main purpose is to provide shade, for it can give little

His only shelter was a bough shed which consisted quite simply of leafy branches laid over poles.

protection from rain or wind. But, as rain falls for only four months of the year, and the sun shines for the rest of the time, he needed no more during the present season.

The dark brown bore-keeper was a quiet, soft-spoken man. He invited us to a drink of tea. His furniture consisted of a rough table of planks over poles on which he kept bags of sugar, flour and packets of tea. His bed was his swag, and his kitchen, the fire-place. We sat about talking and were grateful for the shade and the tea. We repaid his hospitality with cigarettes before we set out on the trail again.

Dick Fallon had asked us to give a lift to a gentleman called Bill who had to go to Leopold Downs to sink a new bore. Bill said he knew the track, but his sense of local geography was blurred by his resort to a last bottle that he had brought with him. We back-tracked when it became apparent that we were on the wrong trail. At last we found ourselves headed for the pass through the limestone range. Poor Bill felt that he had suffered a severe loss of face for his faulty navigation. He kept cursing himself in self-reproach, and it took several more deep draughts of rum to restore his self-esteem. By the time we entered the pass the evening shadows were falling, and the spinifex was glowing in the soft light. The Oscar Range is a low one of broken limestone, and the trail winds through fissured cliffs until it opens out into a flat valley, paved with broken slabs, between which taller spinifex rises high. There are groves of the fantastic baobabs, whose swollen and contorted shapes gave curious aspect to the scene about us. We

Camp of the young boabs

We camped in a clump of young boabs, the trunks of which were still slim and graceful, and as yet undistorted by age.

It was good to stretch out in the arms of Matilda at the end of the day.

camped in a clump of young boabs, the trunks of which were still slim and graceful, and as yet undistorted by age. A clean sandy creek bed, bone dry in this season, made a good camp.

While some of us went out collecting, the others arranged the vehicles, pulled out swags and eating irons, and gathered firewood. It was a beautiful place for a camp. It was good to stretch out in the arms of Matilda at the end of the day, and slowly smoke a cigarette and watch the fiery red of the sunset fade to deep blue while a startlingly bright evening star hung in the sky. As the darkness grew, the firelight lit up the trunks of the trees and made monstrous shapes amongst the branches. This is a wonderful part of the day, that first relaxed hour or so when you make camp and the heat has gone out of the sky. A pipe or cigarette never tastes so good, and a snort of rum in a pannikin seems to ease the tiredness from one's limbs. It is a good time for talk and comradeship, and the first smell of cooking reminds you that you are hungry and adds a pleasant prospect to the hour.

Our talk that night was colourful. Bill revealed a vivid imagination and a descriptive gift to match. He talked much of the northern Kimberleys, a little-known land. And Bill peopled it with creatures that ranged from lion-like to natives seven feet tall.

old Bill the boot sinker.

Bill seemed none the worse for his session at the Fitzroy Crossing.

'I tell yer, fellas, yorter go there.

'Yer never seen nothin' like it.

'There's these great big niggers nobody knows nothin' about.

'Jees, they're like bloody giants. I reckon the lot of 'em 'ull go seven foot high.

'And they reckon, too, that some of 'em wear kinda robes uv some sort. They're not like no other niggers yer never seen.

'I tell yer there's some bloody strange things up there. You zoo blokes ud really see somethin'! No bloody good tellin' yer. You'd never believe a flamin' man. But they're bloody well there all right, youse can bet your bloody boots on it. Then there's them bloody tigers. Nasty bastards with bloody great claws on 'em. They'll go a man at the drop of a hat. Yer won't stand much bloody chance with those buggers. They got teeth on 'em like yore Aunt Martha, and Jees, they can use 'em like her too.

'No good tellin' yer though. Yer gotta see 'em yourself. There's a mass uv bloody stuff yer wouldn't dream about. Yer was asking about bloody black wrens. I don't know nothin' about black wrens, but I've seen a black tit or two in me time. Black wrens. No, but Jees, fellas, you'll see bloody things up there that'll make yer eyes stick out like dogs' balls. I'm not kiddin' yer, I'm dinkum. Yer talk about bloody crocs and bloody 'gators, they're nothin' to the sods yer'll see up there. Jees, they run about thirty and forty foot long, and Christ, are they savage. They'd belt a bullock in one bloody swipe. Youse blokes just wouldn't believe it.'

Bill lapsed into silence and rolled himself a smoke with exaggerated care. Squatting on his haunches with his back against a wheel of the truck, he continued his harangue on the subect of unknown wonders. This eventually wandered off into the business of bore-sinking and finally tailed away altogether as old Bill gave it best and resigned himself to sleep.

Despite the curious creatures that Bill's imagination has so extravagantly created, the fact does remain that those northern areas are little known. Odd tales with the aid of overproof rum and a lively sense of imagery can become campfire legends that give colour and mystique to lives that are so often lonely and drab. It is the fairy tale all over again, complete with monstrous beasts. Bill's chimerical Tiger is not so far removed from Scotland's Loch Ness Monster, the New Guinea Devil Pig, the aboriginal Bunyip, the Kenya Nandi Bear and the Abominable Snow Man of the Sherpa and the mountain romantic. The myths and legends of the aborigines have long populated this land with the shadowy forms of ancestral beings of the Dream Time, part human, part animal, whose pervading presence persists within their minds today. What is a Unicorn or two compared with the Rainbow Snake?

The country beyond the Oscar Range is a plateau paved with rough limestone slabs that lie shattered on the surface of the ground. The crude track that crossed this country made the going slow and tough. It demanded much gear changing, and gave to the trucks an undulating motion like that of small boats running uneasily in a swell. In the blue above, kites swept in long circling glides, tilting languidly in the warm white light of noontide. These hawks were our constant companions. Whenever we glanced upwards they were there on ceaseless patrol. The land was still, save for the gentle movement of the spinifex. Patches of shade beneath the boabs lay like pools of onyx, and in the distance the sky shimmered and the land danced in the clear dry heat. As the day entered the early afternoon the sun shone with a brazen strength, dissipating the pale blue of the morning. Dust rose in vicious swirls as willy-willies sprang up from the surface and skittered across the hot earth, shooting aloft a mess of dry twigs and leaves and spinifex stalks. Here and there a lizard scurried over the rocky ground, a sudden blur of movement that exploded small puffs of dust.

Bill seemed none the worse for his session at the Fitzroy Crossing and now, during the day hours, he again assumed a silence that contrasted with the fertile imagery of his campfire talk. The Leopold Downs homestead was on top of a stony ridge. The track wound past straggling outbuildings and groups of staring aborigines. The attractive children watched wide-eyed as they clutched the cheap cotton skirts of their mothers. Men and women shifted round to gaze impassively as our small convoy drew to a halt in front of the house. We climbed stiffly from the trucks as the manager, a tall young man named Laidlaw, strode over to greet us. We gladly accepted his invitation to a cool drink.

The homestead was the usual station building. It had, as is general, originated from a small, solid one- or two-roomed cottage type building. These were the first permanent shelters erected by the settlers and as the years went by many of them were enlarged so that they came to acquire a rambling character. Houses spread from sheer necessity from such humble beginnings. The environment demanded certain characteristic features such as the addition of verandahs to shade the walls, and a large living-room that

Child at Brown
R.D.G.

The attractive aboriginal children watched wide-eyed.

often has the ease of a common-room. So is evolved a common architectural – if one can use the expression – quality, and a worn and well lived-in atmosphere that gives a feeling of comfort and security amid surroundings that are often harsh and inhospitable. The large and cool living-room that we entered at Leopold has just that quality of comfort and it was extremely pleasant to relax in canvas-slung planter's chairs and put up our feet. Mrs Laidlaw, a charming young Dutchwoman, produced cold drinks and we sat and yarned about the drought, where we had been and where we were heading. Laidlaw told us of the track we were following and of the curious formation of Tunnel Creek and the great caverns that the water had worn in the interior of the range.

126

Men and women gazed as our small convoy drew to a halt.

When it was time to go, he and his wife went into the cold meat-house and cut for us a great slab of fresh beef. This is traditional bush hospitality but we were never any the less grateful for it. We said our goodbyes and our thanks, and climbed back into the trucks. We left in a swirl of dust as the convoy descended the narrow gully, again past the staring groups of station aborigines. At an out-station tank next day we refilled our long-range water-tanks, taking a long and satisfying drink in the meantime. Don Farner duly produced his pills. Then young Tom looked over the top of the tank and found six dead flying foxes.

Don Farner reached for more pills.

Once more we picked our way across the limestone plateau and headed west towards the Precipice Range that in the distance appeared like a wall rising sheer above the flat land. The surface began to break up into rough, dry creeks and the trucks threw up dust clouds so that we kept a good distance between vehicles. We pulled up at one particularly steep and rough-bottomed creek in order to hitch Ivan's big Dodge behind a Land Rover should it be necessary. The Dodge was not equipped with four-wheel drive and it carried a heavy load. But Ivan charged his heavy truck up the broken bank with dash and skill, and we followed more sedately in four-wheel drive.

We assembled around the water bags for a spell. Don Farner took some pills.

Nearby there was a pool of liquid mud, all that remained of a drying waterhole. Lying about were the dead carcases of stock and in the mud was the plastered, bogged body of a calf. Tim discovered it to be still alive. We put a rifle to its head and despatched the poor beast from its misery. Drought is a cruel and pitiless thing and the fear of all who live on the land. Only to the crows and the hawks does it bring the comfort of plenty.

On this creek, as occasionally before, we saw dingo tracks, but never the tawny dingo. All men's hands are turned against the native dog – it is stealthy, cunning and hard to bait or trap. It is a sheep killer and a menace to farmers throughout the length and breadth of the continent. Often it hunts in packs, and it has no natural enemies. The dingo belongs to one of the four non-marsupial groups of mammals that invaded Australia in relatively recent times. The continent was separated from Asia during the Cretaceous, perhaps 100 million years ago. Subsequently bats flew across the seas to Australasia. Rats and mice drifted there on floating logs. Millions of years later the brown men paddled their way there in primitive dugout canoes. And the tawny dog almost certainly came with one of the several waves of these men. The *parvenu* then went bush, and was soon making a good living off the old established families of pouched animals and ground birds. When the white man came with his sheep, the dingo found an easier prey than any that he had hunted during his brief sojourn in Australia.

And so the white man does not like the dingo dog and puts a bounty on his head. The bounty is often substantial. So, specialized men, who do not much care for the company of their fellows, go and live far out by themselves and pit their skill and wits against the innate cunning, and hardly acquired learning, of the wild dog. Victorian shire councils will pay doggers up to forty-five shillings for a dingo's scalp, and in New South Wales the price sometimes goes higher. In Western Australia the rate is generally about a pound and in Queensland they drop thousands of baits from aeroplanes and pay about fifteen shillings for every scalp the dogger brings in. The bounty paid in Western Australia is higher than that in the Northern Territory. It is said that no self-respecting dog ever dies in The Territory – he always crosses the border into W.A.!

We moved on, and found the range rising high to the left of us. The limestone varied in colour from grey to rich rufous. It rose in eroded pinnacles that looked like the battered turrets and bastions of an ancient ruin. The sun began to sink in the western sky and the light glared in through the windscreens. We pulled hat brims down over our eyes and searched the side of the range for the big cleft that we knew would reveal the entrance to the tunnel. At about 3 o'clock in the afternoon we found the dark shadow of the cleft. Shortly after, we got the trucks across the creek that emerged from the rock face. Skirting the trees, we followed the western bank of the dry creek right up into the cool shade of the range, pulling to a halt at the very base of the cliffs.

There in front of us was the opening of the tunnel. It was partly obscured by mighty slabs of fallen stone and the tall leafy trees that grew about the entrance. Here was an ideal camp.

We boiled the billy. Then we climbed down among the giant boulders into the creek bed where it came out of a pitch black tunnel about forty feet broad and high. We got electric torches from the vehicles and waded through cool waters into the cavern. We crossed sand bars, and found the empty shells of crocodile eggs and the footprints of the night herons that fish in the black waters.

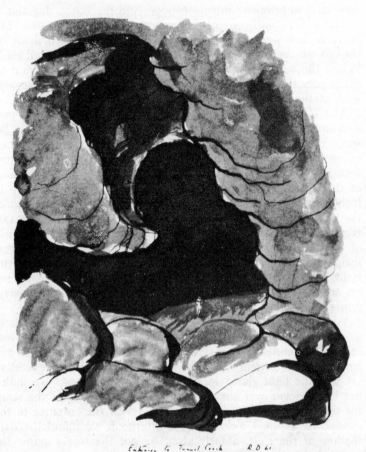

Entrance to Tunnel Creek.   R. D. 61

The tunnel was partly obscured by mighty slabs of fallen stone.

After a hundred yards or so we saw light. We thought that we were on the other side. We were not, though – the light came from a great split in the mountain. We saw the sky through the gash in the range.

Now thousands of clamorous fruit-bats were flapping about us. We went on into new darkness and after several more hundred yards of sand banks and water came again into blinding sunshine.

130

We were now in a hot valley, enclosed on both sides by tall limestone cliffs. Ahead, the dry creek led out to open grassy plains. So secluded was this lovely valley that childhood memories of the stories of Rolf Boldrewood's outlaw, the fictitious Captain Starlight of *Robbery Under Arms*, came irresistibly to mind.

'What a wonderful secret hiding-place this would be for a bushranger!'

It was only when we got back to the other side that one of the others told us this, in fact, was exactly what it had been.

It was once the hiding-place, and the last-ditch stand, of Sandemara, also called Pigeon. In one way, Pigeon was a kind of black William Wallace. He tried to drive the white invader from the land.

Pigeon was a 'black-tracker' in the employ of the Western Australian police in the 'nineties of the last century. On patrol with Constable Richardson he personally captured the notorious Ellemara, a tribal outlaw and cattle spearer of the Kimberleys. But before Pigeon got Ellemara back to Richardson's camp, the captive had persuaded him that black should not be in league with white, and that Pigeon should join Ellemara in a struggle against all Europeans. That night, Pigeon, and another tracker, Captain, murdered the sleeping Richardson. They liberated the prisoners and took to the bush with the guns and ammunition that the white men had taught them to use. They hoped that every aboriginal in the territory would join the movement, and that the white man would be erased from the landscape.

Of course it did not happen that way. By and large, the white men who settled in the area had treated the natives fairly. Pigeon found relatively few volunteers. Worse, other aborigines who were smarting under injustices inflicted by Pigeon (concerned, as usual, with women) joined the whites. Soon, however, Pigeon, Captain and Ellemara ambushed and slaughtered two more white men in Winjana Gorge. These were Burke and Gibbs who, confident in their long friendship with the local tribes, had refused to arm themselves even after hearing of the death of Richardson.

Today this country breathes peace and serenity except for odd times when people like Paddy and Carpenter playfully shoot bullets about the ears of chaps like Harmonious Harry. Sixty years ago Pigeon was planning a coup that involved the slaughter of the police patrol that he knew must follow his latest killing. Pigeon and his mates arranged the bodies of Burke and Gibbs, along with their wrecked waggon and dead horse and bullocks, in a spot

Ellemara, *the rebel.*   R.D. 66

Ellemara, a tribal outlaw of the Kimberleys.

ideal for an ambush. Then for three days the steep red walls of Winjana Gorge echoed with the fire of rifle and shotgun as the outlaws practised shooting for the expected fight.

Ironically, the white patrol was saved by friendly aborigines who told them how to avoid the ambush.

There now came a period of skirmishing in which three white men were wounded and several of the outlaws killed. At one time, it is believed, Pigeon had as many as one hundred men under his command though all but a few were armed only with tribal spears. These men descended on Fossil Downs and nearby stations, spearing cattle and threatening all aborigines who worked contentedly for the whites. Then another white man, Tom Jasper,

Old Rosie. R.fl 61.

Until a few years ago, Pigeon's lubra was still alive.

was shot to death. Once more Pigeon and his men disappeared. It was rumoured that they hid in the depths of unknown limestone caves.

The outlaws displayed singular ingenuity in avoiding the patrols. Further, when they found themselves short of ammunition of a particular calibre, they bound the fine sinews of kangaroos round the cartridges so that they could be wedged tightly into the breaches of other weapons. But, as time went by, more and more of Pigeon's best men were killed or captured – Captain and Ellemara, Lillimore and Demon, Karolan and Tumanurumberi and Long Franky – all these and many others were accounted for, and now Pigeon was almost alone.

His end came at Tunnel Creek, today as full of food – flying foxes, crocodile eggs, night herons and countless long-tailed and zebra finches – as it was in the days of Pigeon. Two patrols led by black trackers converged on the outlaw. He delayed his getaway into the tunnel (with its three outlets) in the hope of getting a close shot at yet another white man. But the patrol shot straighter than he; and in his wounded frenzy Pigeon dropped a parcel of seventeen cartridges, tied up in bark from the paper-bark tree. That left him only three cartridges; and Pigeon died, snarling defiance at the agile black trackers whose bullets finished him off.

Until a few years ago, Pigeon's lubra was still alive.

While some us us were talking over this long-gone history, a small modern tragedy, involving Farner and some flying foxes, was being enacted near the cavern's mouth. Don wanted certain parts of a series of zebra finches. He and his helpers had spread their Japanese mist-nets at the creek's entrance and they sat and smoked, awaiting the coming of the birds. The nets had been set as low as possible so as to trap the finches as they swooped down to the pool to drink. This left a wide opening above the nets and beneath the rocky arch. But it was not low enough.

As the men waited they heard a familiar heavy flapping. Then there was a *whoosh* followed by shrill screaming as three or four bulky fruit-bats hit the delicate mist-net. The chaps raced over the rocks in an attempt to free the animals before they became hoplessly entangled. There followed a form of indoor sport guaranteed to raise a healthy sweat and to produce some really original language. The fruit-bats got themselves into the worst tangle of all time. Flying foxes are equipped with large sharp teeth and these they used. To save the net from being torn to shreds the big bats had to be killed. This ambition was complicated by the fact that nature has endowed the creatures with a pugnacity and will to survival that is out of all proportion to their size. Struggling in what was now darkness, while others directed torch beams from precarious positions on the slippery rock, an attempt was made to garrot the big bats. No amount of choking had the slightest effect on them. In the end, the grisly business was ended by stabbing them to death with knives. This was at last effective, but a gorier and more unseemly *coup-de-grace* could hardly be imagined.

From Tunnel Creek we worked our way westward, stopping at odd places that seemed promising for collections At one outstation, a small tin building, we stopped and had a drink of tea with a couple of stockmen. We sat in a bough shed that did duty as a kind of outdoor living-room. It was furnished simply with a rough table, camps beds and kerosene cases to sit on. Pleasant quiet men, they were pleased to have company. Tea was produced in a black iron teapot and we drank from stained and battered pannikins. It was hot, strong and good. Walking about the table and the camp beds with great aplomb was a white corella, the common cockatoo of the north-west. These are engaging birds. Pure white and with a light blue ring about the eyes, they are indefatigable comedians and mimics. This character took a great fancy to one of us who made a fuss of him while we sat yarning. He walked about our arms and shoulders, nuzzling and chattering in a hoarse whiskey voice. One of the men laughed when told that we had given Bill a lift to Leopold Downs.

'Bill's a good old bloke,' he said.

'And a bloody good bore-sinker. But he likes to hit the turps now and again, and you can't blame him. It's hard work sinking bores, and after a few months on your own, with no one but a coupla abos to yarn to, you've gotta get stinkin' once in a

Pleasant, quiet men, they were pleased to have company.

while. I reckon it's only natural. Bill's a great bloke to yarn when he's full. Some of the things he comes out with 'd knock the arse out of a rag-doll, he's that funny. Aw, he's not a bad bloke, Bill.'

At Winjana Gorge we found the wide and sandy entrance littered with sun-dried carcases of cattle that had been bogged in what were now waterless hollows. Upstream there was water in plenty, and the gorge rang with the song of birds. The rock walls rose high on either side, and the heat reflecting from rock and sand turned us back to the welcome shade of the timber. This is where Pigeon and his men slaughtered Burke and Gibbs. Ivan

'Bill's a good old bloke,' he said.

drew our attention to a dead and mangled snake. A yard or two away lay the body of a feral cat. The remains of another savage battle fought at Winjana.

We were always vaguely on the lookout for the taipan, a rather disagreeable snake that occurs in southern New Guinea and northern Australia but which has not yet been found in the Kimberleys. The taipan, like most snakes, is extremely shy but, when cornered, it can strike with a rapidity that is disconcerting. It grows to a length of seven or eight feet. Because of the length of its fangs, and the capacity of its poison lakes, only one or two people have ever recovered from its bite.

We met with no taipans, nor other big snakes for that matter. We saw a few small ones here and there, but as usual, these sensed us first and quickly got out of our way. Some people say that snakes hear you coming but, despite the snake charmer, his cobra and his pipe, snakes cannot hear in the usual vertebrate manner. They have no auditory apparatus capable of perceiving air-borne vibrations. There is no external ear opening and a middle ear is virtually absent. But they do have a complete and delicate connection between their under-surface, touching the ground, and their inner ears, and footfalls and other vibrations (such as the tap of the snake charmer's foot) are instantly appreciated by the serpent's brain. And so they can get out of the way quickly. Most species usually do so before an ordinary noisy, booted person is close enough to see them.

We returned to Broome via Kimberley Downs and Derby. At Meda the Wells very kindly fed us, let us use their showers and showed us bower-birds gambolling in the garden a yard or so from their homestead verandah. We reached Derby in the late afternoon and made straight for the post-office and mail. This we took to the pub. We read our letters over the first cold beer that we had had since we left Fossil Downs. Derby is a small, straggling town on King Sound into which runs the Fitzroy River. From here cattle are shipped out to Perth and Singapore. Many of the houses have attractive gardens, and trees grow about the town. The town trees include some of the biggest baobabs we have seen. One of them is locally celebrated not merely for its enormous girth, but because its hollow trunk was used in the early days as the town *boob*. Its cavernous hollow easily accommodated several prisoners. Flying about the town were the usual flocks of white corellas, and as they moved in the baobabs they gave the trees the appearance of suddenly bursting into flower.

The pub is a pleasant, rather shambling old building with verandahs about it where you can sit in the shade and watch the frost gather on the tall schooners.

Apart from the big hollow bottle tree there is little in Derby today to remind us of the town's tempestuous past. The coastal inlets here were surveyed by *Beagle*, and the Fitzroy River was named by Commander John Lort Stokes after a former turbulent skipper, the man, in fact, who considered disqualifying the young Charles Darwin from the job of Naturalist because he disapproved of the shape of Darwin's nose. In 1838, a party from the *Beagle* ascended the Fitzroy for about twenty-two miles until they found the channel choked by debris. It was not until 1879 that Alexander Forrest explored the plains of the Fitzroy and reported on the richness of the soil and the suitability of the country for grazing. The first pioneers began to move in shortly afterwards. These men created epics of fortitude and endurance that have become legends of the cattle camps. Men like Nat Buchanan, who took the first mob of cattle into the Ord, and the Duracks, and the MacDonald brothers.

At the mouth of the Fitzroy River the settlers established a small cattle landing where the town of Derby was later to arise. Then, in 1885, suddenly gold was discovered at Hall's Creek. The far-off Kimberleys were brought to the attention of the nation and the 'Trail of '86' was on. Charlie Hall and Jack Slattery made the actual strike. The rush of '86 brought 10,000 men, women and children pouring through the Kimberleys during the few short years of the field's existence. To all the elements of cruelty, greed, lust and murder of a rush was added the dreadful toll in human lives that the long road took. Men died of thirst, of starvation, and of death at the hands of vengeful natives from whom a fearful punishment was exacted. During these desperate few years the natives paid with their lives for their attempts to repel the invaders. At Hall's Creek a shanty town sprang up. The creeks and gullies echoed with the ring of pick and shovel and nights were rent by the raucous sound of miners on the rum.

They came from everywhere by two main routes. By schooner and bark and brigantine through Derby and the new port of Wyndham, from Adelaide along the Overland Telegraph Line to The Katherine, and then west across from The Territory. The inland trails were marked with the refuse of broken bottles, discarded rags of clothing and the smashed trappings of an urban existence as though left by a disordered army in retreat. For thousands it was a march through hell with no reward at the end of it.

When the news came of a flash strike hundreds of miles to the west, there was another ambitious rush towards the setting sun. Now the little bag and slab villages in the Hall's Creek gullies were deserted and forgotten, and once more the ancient solitude descended like the noonday heat. Life lingered on in the main settlement, for the more substantial character of its dwellings encouraged those too tired or old, to settle and seek no further the rainbow's end. So, as we saw on our visit to Rob Moody, it became a small and useful township, supplying the needs of far-away cattle stations, and assuaging the loneliness of wayfarers, or those who come in for relaxation from a hard and solitary life in the bush.

Today the gold is gone, and the mainstay of the Kimberleys is the export of beef cattle. Great numbers of beasts are driven hundreds of miles to the meatworks, with a resultant loss of condition that militates against quality and price. Nowadays, at Glenroy, one of the more distant properties, cattle in their prime are slaughtered on the station. The carcases are then flown out to the port of Wyndham. This air-beef scheme, as it is called, works well. Carcases are carried aboard Dakota and Bristol air-freighters and are hooked up on racks that run the length of the fuselage. A government subsidy, and the increased price brought by prime beef, offsets the cost of air transportation.

We left Derby and headed south. It was good to be on the road to Broome again. The shade temperature that day was 109 degrees at noon, and the light was almost blinding. We pulled up to yarn with an old station hand who was making his way through the pindan scrub to a watering place. Before taking a drink from the proffered water bag, he pulled off his wide-brimmed hat and filled it with water from our rear water-tank. He let his horse drink its fill. Then he himself had a drink. He was one of the old type bushmen. Lean and hard, with a grey stubble of beard on his lined face, his eyes were screwed up against the light. His hands, thin and bony, with skin like tanned leather, deftly rolled a cigarette while he talked to us in a slow drawl. Like many men in the outback he gave the impression that he had known us a long time and that he was merely carrying on a conversation that we had been having last week. No questions, just yarning, and taking for granted that we were there for our own good reasons that were no concern of his. After a while he straightened up and pulling his

139

hat over his eyes said, 'Well I reckon a man'd better make tracks or he won't make the bore before dark. Thanks for the water.'

And he swung himself up on to his horse, raised a hand and rode slowly away through the pindan.

13

After our previous rush through the town it was pleasant to be able to linger awhile with the Souths at the Governor Broome Hotel. There were showers. We drank quantities of cold Swan as we boiled up our appallingly dirty clothes in the copper out at the back of the pub. In the evenings we went to the pub dances. Leaning on the bar we talked to Japanese pearl divers, Malay boys, truck drivers, officials and drifters and got the feel of the place. Also drinking in the G.B. bar was a hard-looking, though not unattractive little hybrid person called Norah. She surreptitiously threw small fireworks to amuse the men, and to annoy a tough stringy blonde a good many years older than herself. We bought Norah some beer, and then she ran out of matches. We lit her fireworks, first making her promise that we should share the same cell if we all went to jail for disturbing the peace. We learnt later that there was no need to extract any such promise. She was locally celebrated as Nopants Norah.

Norah, we were told, was almost perennially *enceinte,* and was the resigned mother of a brood that involved a wide spectrum of the male elements of the community. The kindly Mrs South, tolerant to a degree concerning the peccadillos of others, felt nevertheless a tinge of sadness when Norah was once more revealed to be in a certain condition.

'Oh, Norah,' she said quietly, 'it's happened again. Who was it this time?'

'Mrs South,' replied Norah, 'if you'd been cut by a circular saw, would *you* know which tooth did the damage?'

It is said, nostalgically, that Broome's best days have gone. But although the settlement needs a shave, it is still the fascinating rapscallion town that we had read about ever since we were children. There is no other place quite like it – a colourful seaport of graceful luggers in mangrove creeks, of shimmering tin roofs, with cheerful crowds of divers from all over the pearling seas. These, and the native aborigines, and hybrids, far out-number the white population who are themselves recruited from throughout the seven seas. In the bell-bottomed boab trees around the town perch hundreds of dusty white corellas – blue-faced cockatoos that contend with the local domestic fowls at feeding times. The corellas are so much an accepted part of Broome that the fowls are given double rations to make up for them.

Broome is the only place we know where you can buy a Beach-comber's Licence. We almost bought a couple, but the cost was £4 a year, and we were hard up at the time. It is an official

The luggers go a-pearling in the calm season.

government document authorising the bearer to gather pearl and other materials washed up on the beach. It forms a loose kind of control over various odd characters in an area where it is too easy to steal shell from the sheds along the shores of the bay.

We visited the shell-sheds and the luggers on the mangrove creeks along the foreshores. The luggers go a-pearling in the calm season and come home to 'lay-up' during the wild cyclonic storms that may occur from November and December to April.

Pearling in Western Australia began about 1861. It was started, oddly enough, by an American sailor. This gentleman, named Tays, saw the commercial value of the pearl-shell lying about the inshore reefs. He employed aborigines to help him gather it. At first the shell was so abundant that it could be picked up by men wading about the reefs. It is said that pickle-bottles full of pearls were bought from aboriginal collectors for a pound or two of coarse tobacco. This is only perhaps an exaggeration. Then, when the inshore pearl shell petered out, Malay divers were recruited to get it up out of the shallows. When it became rare there, the lugger came into its own, with Japanese and Malay divers working from ports like Cossack and Broome out to the distant grounds of the Indian Ocean.

Of all divers, Japanese are the most successful. Temperamentally, too, they are superior; they can live amicably for long periods in the cramped quarters of smelly luggers. At sea the massive pearl oyster is cleaned from the shell. Its muscle is given to the crew as a perquisite. This is sun-dried in the rigging, and it forms the basis of an outstanding curry. The occasionally found pearls are put into the ship's pearl box. When the lugger comes in with her cargo of plate-sized, gold-lipped shell, the odd pearls are sold to buyers and ultimately reach Paris and other European centres.

Perhaps more interesting than ordinary pearls, though far less valuable today, are those locally known as 'barrack'. This expression is a corruption of 'baroque'. 'Barrack' pearls may be of fantastic shapes. They are sometimes formed by pearly deposits over fishes, crabs, and other small marine animals that have invaded the shell and died there. Often they have to be punched free from the shell to which they are attached.

The great days of the baroque pearl were before even the Dutch found these shores. In the Italian Renaissance the master jewellers, and their fastidiously discriminating clientele, prized above most things the individualistic and the eccentric in gemstone and pearl. Pendants in particular provided a medium in which baroque pearls show to advantage. According to its individual irregularities, a pearl could be used for the lustrous body, or some other part, of a mermaid, a hippocamp, an angel or, in fact, any classical or other object within the inspiration of the jeweller. Gold, gemstones and enamel were used to provide heads, tails and other appendages or embellishments.

Today there is little demand for the eccentric, or even the individual, in pearl or gemstone. The wife of the successful real

Of all divers, the Japanese are the most successful.

estate spiv or take-over specialist wants a string of perfectly graded pearls. She wants a square emerald, or a large hard, brilliant-cut piece of white 'rock'.

Around the pubs we heard much talk of pearls, some of it no doubt true. We heard of the lustrous Star of the West, 'as big as a sparrow's egg', that was worth £6,000 in 1917. We heard of the Blaxall Pearl, found on the other side of Australia, and allegedly valued at £20,000. We were informed that it is now a 'priceless part of the Crown jewels'. We were solemnly told, too, that the famous Southern Cross was 'found on the beach near Broome among the seaweed' by a youth who sold it for £10 and a bottle of rum. We asked what would be the current price of the Southern Cross; and where was it today? The chaps guessed that it is worth at least £25,000, and declared that it is in the Vatican Collection, bought by Roman Catholic subscription and presented to a pope in the twenties of the present century. Was the Vatican 'sold a pup', or, rather, presented with one (see p. 79 *et seq.*)?

How true are some of these tales we cannot say. They are the things we talked about in the bars of Broome.[1]

Although a single pearl, then, may fetch several thousand pounds, the real profits nonetheless come from shell. Inevitably, modern plastics have knocked the bottom out of the industry. A palliative is the recent development of a local cultured pearl industry. We were told by Broome dealers that north-western pearls now produced are superior to any other and that the Japanese, who discovered the means of pearl culture, were investing in the local industry.

So there was much talk of pearl culture. We heard of the Japanese wizard, Mikimoto, who, it is said, was the first to 'farm' artificially induced pearls in the eighties of the last century. At the age of twenty-three, Mikimoto concluded that the local pearling beds would soon be fished out. He talked of trying to grow pearls.

'You can grow turnips,' the sceptics are alleged to have told him, 'but not pearls.'

He began to experiment by introducing artificial objects – pottery beads, tiny glass globules and the like – into the shells. He had no success. Then he tried fragments of pearl-shell and obtained some distorted semi-circular growths. By the end of the

[1] The Vatican was *not* sold a pup. The Southern Cross is in private hands in London, S.W.3.

145

century he was wrapping living oyster tissue round his introduced objects and triumphantly producing globular pearls. He had begun a great new industry. Later, westerners tried to compete by the production of shoddy artificial pearls that had never seen the sea. There is a story that the now ageing Mikimoto, in anger and dismay, bought 25,000 dollars worth of these. Then he put them into a furnace, fearing that their miserably poor quality would detract from the sale of his cultured sea pearls.

There was much talk of a new, Japanese-financed cultured pearl industry north of Derby, but people were vague about details. It was only after we left the area that the news burst into the press. A choker of north-western pearls made £45,000 in New York. The centre pearl alone was valued at £5,000, and it was reported that individual pearls worth £1,800 to £2,000 have now become relatively commonplace. The site of this new industry is Kuri Bay, about 200 miles north of Broome. This place is accessible only by lugger and it was named after Mr Kuribayashi the president of Pearls Pty Ltd, the company that is exploiting its waters. It is said that the locally cultured pearls have a silvery-pink sheen that is unique; and that they grow much bigger than do cultured pearls anywhere else, bigger almost, than local natural pearls. In Japan, the oysters used for pearl culture are a mere three or four inches in diameter; in the north-west, up to a foot. It takes about five years for the growth of a pearl to a diameter of one quarter of an inch in Japanese waters. A pearl may reach a lustrous half an inch in as little as two years in Kuri Bay.

The pearlers around the pubs told us that the warmth of the tropical waters and the enormous north-western tide-wash were chiefly responsible for the faster growth of the local pearls. Perhaps these are, in fact, significant subsidiary factors. Whether beneficial or not in the formation of pearls, the dangerously swift rise and fall of the local tides have excited respect and comment from earliest times. Dampier wrote of them, and was led to believe that a strait, or at least a large river, must be somewhere near. King's little vessel *Mermaid* was picked up in the tide-rip during a dead calm but 'happily . . . swept passed the rocks without accident'. She was carried on yet another half mile and passed several islands at no more than thirty yards distance at a rate of eight or nine knots.

Besides getting the most shell, the Japanese occupy the biggest and best-kept part of the lonely bush cemetery a few miles beyond the town. Each separate language group – Chinese, Malay,

146

Japanese and European – has its own characteristic style of grave furnishings. The Malayan graves are the most casual. They are decorated with a handful of shells and a raised border of inverted sunken beer bottles. The Australian graves, well, they are like European graves anywhere; and their marble headstones are shipped in from Perth, 2,000 miles south. The Chinese graves march in military precision, concrete-sealed, symmetrically decorated and, in some cases, covered with aluminium paint. For the convenience of mourners, there stands nearby a small tin shed. This is surrounded by the discarded empty cases (not merely bottles) of Swan lager, potent evidence, if you like, of the high spirits with which the Broome Chinese see off their friends.

By contrast, the Japanese divers have, in a curiously humble way, introduced the charm of a peasant art. Their headstones are rough plinths of local stone pleasantly cut with characters extolling the person below. At funerals, food and beer (in lieu of wine) are left on the grave for the departed spirit. The less reverent coloured townsfolk find this a source of free grog after the retirement of the mourners. So the Japanese have taken to embedding the beer-bottles in concrete. It is said that the locals, not to be denied their natural rights, suck up the beer through straws.

When the tide was low Eunice South guided us to the footprints of dinosaurs in the sandstone of Gantheaume Point. These possibly bird-like dinosaurs stalked along what was a sandy beach in Jurassic times. Their footprints had sunk into sand that was firm enough to leave sharp impressions. Then before their walls caved in, the depressions were filled with other material: the original footprints acted as a mould. Next, the whole was overlain and millions of years later this upper stratum, including the contents of the footprints, was eroded away. So the sharp-etched dinosaur tracks remain, after 120 million years of change in the surrounding countryside.

Although all dinosaurs were developed from a single reptile stock, two very widely different kinds arose. One group had a hip structure like that of today's birds. From reptiles of this affinity modern birds have arisen. It is, perhaps, a sobering thought that the robin in your garden has in its skeleton, and elsewhere, features that reveal its distant relationship with one kind of dinosaur.

The second kind of dinosaur had a hip structure of a kind that still persists in modern lizards, crocodiles and turtles. These dinosaurs with the lizard-like hips ranged in size from reptiles little bigger than collie dogs to fantastic meat-eating creatures about fifty feet long, including their armoured, lashing tails, and to even larger, vegetarian dinosaurs, perhaps almost always supported partly by the water of the swamps in which they grazed, that sometimes grew as long as eighty feet and weighed as much as forty tons. A considerable size-range (but not as great) also existed in the bird-hipped dinosaurs. In some huge dinosaurs the brain was scarcely bigger than a walnut. The spinal enlargements controlling the movement of the massive, pillar-like legs and lashing tail were sometimes twenty times as big as the true brain.

It would be the merest speculation to suggest the kind of dinosaur that made the footprints on the coast at Broome. Both main groups – whatever their hip structure – contained families that possessed bird-like feet. A fragment of hip or jaw would settle the problem at once, but there is no certainty that such relics will be discovered. The exposed sandstone beds here are about forty feet thick. Bores have shown that below there lies another great formation about 900 feet thick, and beneath this, a substantial deposit of Jurassic silt. Locked within this massive, rigid coffin there no doubt exist the mineralised bones of countless dinosaurs and other Mesozoic animals. Whether they will ever be seen by man is another question.

In these Mesozoic times – the great 'mid-period' of animal development between say, 200 and 60 million years ago – dinosaurs ranged, some sorts in herds, over most of the earth The first positively described as a reptile came from Sussex. Dinosaurs reached Australia from the north while the continent was still attached to Eurasia by land bridges. In Australia they faded, comparatively suddenly, just as they did elsewhere. Yet they lived for a space of about 100 million years. Man has been here for perhaps three-quarters of a million years. As the American palaeontologist Colbert has said: Who are *we* to say that the dinosaurs were unsuccessful?

At Broome we varied our routine visits to post-office and public house with one to the bank. The traveller in Australia finds his occasional transactions at bush or other banks as pleasant and easy an interlude as it is in England. One has never yet been inside an American bank (nor consulate, for that matter) without leaving in ill-humour. The servants of banks (and consulates) in the United States seem to assume from the outset that the traveller is there solely with criminal intent. Australian banks, following British tradition (this time, an excellent one), assume that the traveller who signs his name a little differently, or who has mislaid his letter of credit, is not necessarily a crook but merely a bit of a *nong* who should be put in funds and told gently to try not to do it again. Parenthetically, it should be explained that a nong is a gentleman with only three cerebral cells. One works clockwise, the other anti-clockwise, and so the poor fellow has only one grey cell to see him through.

In one respect, however, Australian banking practice falls far short of that in Britain. This is an indulgence in nasty little 'exchange' tricks that have about them a whiff of rank dishonesty. In the colonial days, and particularly during the gold-rushes, banks ran a very considerable risk of losing bullion when stage coaches were 'stuck-up' by bushrangers. It is said (although we do not know whether this is true or not) that, as a form of insurance, banks began to charge 'exchange' on intercolonial drafts. After Federation, the colonies became states. Today, Australian banks still persist in exacting a 7s. 6d. fee per £100 as 'exchange' on a Sydney cheque tendered in Broome, and 2s. 6d. on any draft that crosses a border. A parallel situation in Britain to the latter example would be a bank charge of 2s. 6d. in Edinburgh on lodgement of a cheque issued in Newcastle. Even if one wishes to send a few shillings between the local equivalents of say London and Reading, Australian banks remorselessly extract a miserable little sixpenny fee. In short, they indulge in an unscrupulous and petty little bushranging trick of their own. And the traveller has no means of escape.[1]

From Broome our route led south. We would go down the Madman's Track towards the old Kalgoorlie goldfields and thence across the Nullarbor Plain back to eastern Australia. First, we had to retrace our earlier route of about 400 miles between Broome and Port Hedland. Apart from Anna Plains, and one or two other station homesteads, there is nothing along this lead apart from the Pardoo Sands and the stretch of Eighty Mile Beach. We wanted to camp for a night on this mighty beach. Here the prevailing winds from the Central Desert Basin spill the desert right to the edge and into the Timor Sea.

Late in the afternoon we left the Pardoo Sands track and headed seawards. We got the lurching vehicle right over to the first line of dunes. It was a strange sight from the top of these naked sandhills. As far as we could see in either direction there was a

---

[1] They have since given up this nasty little habit.

broad stretch of fine white sand that merged into the horizon. This Eighty Mile Beach seemed to us to be one of the loneliest places in the world. The very high rise and fall of the ocean tide takes the water out for miles so that we gazed seawards over what looked like a flat, glistening plain. There are no near off-shore reefs, so, when the water rushes shorewards on the rising tide, an immense variety of shells are rolled in and piled in thousands of tons along the shore. From great pink baler and lamp shells to tiny polished cowries, they lie like a glittering carpet. To the eyes of a child this would seem one vast Aladdin's cave of treasures. Some of us felt a childish urge to start gathering specimens. But as fast as we picked up a shell, an even better one one was seen. Because there are no rocks, a large percentage of the shells come ashore undamaged. Choosing and discarding, the laymen of the party sated the appetites of boyhood's dream of treasure trove.

Sometimes we saw cone shells. Altlough we knew that the animals that made them were dead, there was always with us a reflex hesitation before picking them up. For, apart from sea-snakes, sharks and crocodiles, and the big groper that sometimes attacks pearl divers, these northern seas contain only two hazards, and both belong to the reefs. One is the stone fish, an ugly knobbly creature that has hollow spines surmounting poison glands. These discharge up into the feet of incautious waders and cause intense agony, and sometimes death. The other danger is this lovely patterned *Conus* that we were now picking up along the Eighty Mile Beach.

There are many species of *Conus*, but perhaps only two big ones are known to kill man. These animals lurk under submerged coral debris, and if their pretty shells are handled carelessly they will shoot out a barb which makes a tiny puncture into which is thrust poison from a gland below. We were in no danger. The gastropods that made the shells were dead before they were washed ashore. The flesh and the poison had long ago washed away. Only the delicately patterned, slightly barrel-shaped, shells remained for us to admire.

Patrolling the beach were scores of the wading birds that oscillate in great migratory flights between Australia and Siberia. We were in the middle of spring. Were these birds some that had missed last autumn's nuptial flight to the Asiatic summer, and had perforce spent a celibate winter in Australia, or had they just returned from breeding on the northern tundras? Dom, who knows about these things, was not with us at this particular camp. Ivan, too, had left us to drive direct south, and home. So we consulted The Book, or as we sometimes called it, *The Word*. This is Serventy and Whittell's *Birds of Western Australia* which is, unhappily, the only scholarly thing of its kind in Australia. The Good Book told us that the breeding exodus northward from this coast begin in mid-April, and that the return of the post-nuptial migrants is apparent from the beginning of September onwards. The odds, then, were that the many long-winged waders in front of us now had just completed their 8,000-odd mile southern journey. They would spend the summer with us. Then off they would go again, to another cooler, greener summer on the northern steppes.

We had noticed the tracks of some kind of small creature leading from the beach up over the steep dunes and back into low scraggy plant growth beyond. We followed one such track inland for about a hundred yards. We were astonished to find that it was made by a small hermit crab which seemed to have laboriously dragged itself and its sea-shell armour the whole of that distance. We wondered why these creatures performed such long journeys. On the smooth steep banks of the dunes we found many such tracks. Often the tiny travellers had slipped and slithered down the banks, only to start once more on their obscure but urgent journey.

Until the sun went down beneath the Timor Sea we were plagued by clouds of nasty little native flies. These seem to be able to breed in any sort of organic matter and so far nobody has found any successful means of combating them, especially as they rarely go indoors. Dampier did not like them either and, as so often, he had an original comment for the situation: 'Without the assistance of both hands to keep them off, they will creep into one's Nostrils; and Mouth too, if the Lips are not shut very close.' And of the fly-pestered aborigines: 'So that, from their Infancy being thus annoyed by these Insects, they do never open their Eyes, as other People: and therefore they cannot see far; unless they hold up their Heads, as if they were looking at somewhat over them. They have great Bottle noses . . . They have no Houses, but lye in the open Air, without any covering; the Earth being their Bed, and the Heaven their Canopy.'

Firewood was scarce but we found enough dead shrubs to make a fire sufficiently big to boil up the billy for tea. We unrolled our Matildas between the dunes. People who have never slept on sand

We were glad to run out of The Pardoo and into the small shattered rock hills that appear before you come to Port Hedland.

generally say it makes a soft and pleasant bed. It does not. It packs below you as hard as a rock.

At night the wind blew up. It filled our swags with sand. We were still far above the Tropic of Capricorn but the night was chill in the biting wind. It was still blowing strongly when we woke next morning, but we gladly put up with it because it made the flies leave us alone. We shook as much of the sand out of our gear as we could, and put the Land Rover into low ratio and crawled back across the dunes to the road. We were pleased that we had put in a night's camp on the Eighty Mile Beach, but one such night would be enough for some years. We calculated that we could do the two hundred miles to Port Hedland and be fifty miles further on along the Woodstock track by late afternoon. The day grew hotter, and the wind kept sweeping clouds of sand across the road ahead. We were glad to run out of The Pardoo, and into the small shattered rock hills that appear before you come to Port Hedland.

Approached from the north, the town of Port Hedland comes rather as a surprise after flat and arid Pardoo land. It sprawls about a good deal, but there are trees in the streets and some pleasant old stone buildings help to give the town a substantial air. We made straight for the pub and cooled off in the bar. As far as we could gather from the notice board, Billy the Lurk was no longer under the Dog Act. Either his time had run out or

Whispering Smith had relented. A neighbouring drinker overhead our conversation and discovered that we had started out from Sydney. He said he had just flown across the continent and back for a holiday.

'How did you like the Big Smoke?' we asked.

'Or, she's orright.'

'What do you mean, orright?'

'Or, she's orright, but she's not much chop fer an 'oliday.'

'What do you mean she's not much chop fer an 'oliday?'

'Well I mean she's orright and she aint orright.'

'Why aint she orright?'

'Well she's orright, but yer can't get a flamin' drink before seven in the mornin'.'

Twelve miles east of Port Hedland the road branches south to Woodstock. To most of us the track was new. This is flat spinifex country, with sandy red soil running in low undulations to the horizon. As the sun sank, the country began to glow. In the distance granite extrusions appeared, split and weathered out into tumbles of boulders, deep red in the failing evening sun. The clarity of the light was magnificent. Each rock and scrubby tree stood out sharp and distinct, and the sky turned to a translucent blue that gave way to a fiery gold on the skyline.

Here and there motionless kangaroos sat staring, poised in the attitude that presages flight. The fading light emphasized the startling white of their briskets. Erect on their splayed hind legs and tails, staring warily with small forepaws held out as though to parry an uncertain danger, they would suddenly wheel about and go off in great bounds for the shelter of the rocks. We camped on the bank of a dry sandy creek that gave us plenty of good firewood. Although the day had been hot, the evening, as usual, was cool. But a good big log will burn all night if you find the right timber. Fresh bread, a rarity, and the steak bought in Port Hedland, went down pretty well. The night was still and the sky blazed with stars. We lay in our swags yarning, looking forward to next day's visit to the biological station at Woodstock Station.

Next morning we called in at Abydos Station where we were made welcome with tea on a pleasant wide verandah. We could never quite lose our surprise at arriving out of arid wilderness to find ourselves in the midst of a shady country garden, green and colourful with lawns and flowers, and to sit relaxed exchanging news with a charming and coolly frocked hostess. It was only at these times that we became conscious of our travel stains. Good china, too, always seemed a bit ethereal after tea-stained pannikins.

And so we came back to Woodstock – a different Woodstock from that which Oxfordshire knows. No doubt some nostalgic Oxonian travelled through this remote place in the nineteenth century and called it so. The Western Australian Woodstock is situated in a plain from which rear giant granite extrusions that suggest that a stupendous bulldozer had piled rock on rock in pryamidal steps. We had been told that these tumbled rocks are incised with the art of long-gone men, and later we were delighted to find that this is so.

We crossed the broad sandy bed of a creek and came to the old homestead. This creek only runs after rains and so at other times water is obtained from bores. In the 'eighties, when gold was discovered thereabouts, the bui ding was originally put up as a pub. Solidly made of stone it is a cool and pleasant place.

The old homestead was deserted for many years but is now owned by the Department of Agriculture and was currently bursting with life. It had been lent to the Commonwealth Scientific and Industrial Research Organisation which had set up a research station for the study of the biology of the euro, a large wallaby, or small kangaroo, that ranges in great numbers through the north-west.

The Officer-in-Charge was Tim Ealey. Ealey is a short, thickset man in his thirties, with a pleasant, relaxed manner that puts a stranger at ease in a matter of moments. Comfortably dressed in an old khaki shirt, shorts and dusty desert boots he typifies the young ecologist of today who is adding so much to our scientific knowledge in rough and out of the way places. Ealey had a crew of young men like himself who spent their nights patrolling the surrounding country in a Land Rover and wrestled with bucking and biting 'roos in the dust of the wire-fenced compound in which the animals were trapped. The atmosphere was rather like the cameraderie of a horsebreaker's camp where men may sit about amiably yarning and who, next moment, are engaged in violent and strenuous exertion.

The old homestead at Woodstock is a rambling building made of local rock. It became a station homestead when the gold cut out and the country was given over to sheep. Now there are no sheep. The place has been taken over by wallabies, goannas and scientists.

The big front room had been converted into a cool and com-

Donald Farner examining a goanna. R.B.

The place has been given over to wallabies, goannas and scientists. Don Farner examines a small goanna.

fortable common room with a kitchen at one end. This was furnished simply enough with cane chairs in which the men could sprawl with magazines and cool drinks after a day's work, and before the labours of the evening began. Woodstock is a region that can be really hot with the summer shade temperature standing in the hundreds for weeks on end.

Ealey and his team were engaged on an exceedingly interesting job of applied biology. It had to do with the local decline in sheep numbers for which the euro was alleged to be responsible. So the Wildlife Survey Section of the C.S.I.R.O., which has an outstanding research record in relation to rabbit control by means of myxomatosis, and in other matters, undertook to try to discover just where the euro stood in relation to the diminishing numbers of that sacred animal, *Ovis aries*, the domestic sheep.

That the sheep was not doing too well in the Pilbara area is indisputable. Here six stations had been abandoned and, according to local sheep-farmers, a dozen more were in a precarious state.

Ealey told us that if these, too, had to be surrendered, about 10 million acres of once fairly good country would fall idle. The reason for the decline of the flocks seemed fairly clear: the more nutritious native pastures were no longer regenerating themselves. and it is these grasses, and other high-protein plants, that the ewes in particular need for the development of their unborn young and for the production of the milk on which the lambs later depend. The big problem was what caused the good herbage to fade and to be replaced by relatively unpalatable invaders such as buck spinifex, poverty-bush and the like.

Two reasons were given by local sheep-farmers. They claimed that first, 'poor seasons' were responsible. But examination of past weather records by a young Dutch agriculturist, Henk Suijdendorp, showed that a big decline had taken place in the numbers of sheep some years before and during a period of unprecedentedly high rainfall. The sheep-farmers claimed, secondly, that the number of euros increased sharply when water supplies on the stations were artifically improved and that the marsupials than ate up the pastures and deprived the sheep of the best sustenance.

Tom Ealey handling a Euro.   R. D. '61

When it was grabbed the chap had a fairly positive proposition on his hands.

Tim Ealey was sent out to try to assess the importance of the euro as a competitor of the sheep, and, if need be, to discover the best means of controlling it.

One night we went out with a group on their routine operations. The euro always feeds in the cool of the evenings. By so doing it conserves vital body fluids without which it would rapidly die from heat-exhaustion. The Woodstock area was surveyed and divided into working areas on a grid pattern. The boundaries of these areas were marked off with posts that bore numbered reflectors so that they could be quickly and easily identified in the headlights or by spotlight at night. At one place, a fence-trap had been set around a well so that when a 'roo came to water he could find his way in but could not get out. At other wells the euros were free to move in and out but as they left they were automatically counted by a *kangarometer* and at the same time indelibly marked with dye for future identification.

During the night the fence-trap was examined and the imprisoned 'roos examined. This entailed real work. A mature euro may weight about one hundred pounds and when it was grabbed the chaps had a fairly positive proposition on their hands. The best method is to grab the beast by the tail, envelop it with a heavy net, and then bring it to the ground and wrap a bag over its head. While it was held down, Ealey could record its size by foot and tail-length, and then, after removal of the bag, determine its age by inspection of the state of its tooth development. Finally, a yellow plastic collar, inscribed with a luminous number that could be read by night, was put around the euro's neck. The 'roo was then released. In this way the group could easily identify individuals encountered in the bush. During the course of five years' work, hundreds of animals were recorded and many individual territories defined. The euro was found to be a sedentary animal, sharply limited to a territory of just a few hundred yards.

Standing in the back of the Land Rover, we drove along the grid tracks. playing the lights over the surrounding grasslands. Whenever a 'roo was sighted Ealey checked the collar-number through field glasses while an assistant in the front seat would make the record. Tim would then say, 'Righto – run on to 4 Division. At 4 we'll find Old 87 feeding near the boundary line.'

Sure enough, as we reached the reflector showing the 4 Division boundary post, 'Old 87' was found there. He sat uneasily in the glare, looking rather like a small boy caught stealing jam. Further on would be others, singly or in pairs and always where Tim predicted they would be. Uncollared animals were noted as well. It is not surprising that this group of men got the required answers.

The essential cause of the trouble was mismanagement of the pastures as suggested by Suijdendorp even before the euro work began. Ealey and his people found that the increasing number of euros has little or nothing to do with it. It was found that in areas where there had always been a natural plentitude of water, over-stocking had produced the same result. When Suijdendorp experimented with a certain density of sheep in euro-proof enclosures, the same pasture changes occurred. Under a ratio of a mere one sheep continually grazing over four acres, there was no season regeneration of grassland: the natural herbage simply cannot stand this perennial assault by sheep. Again, when sheep-farmers burnt off areas in an attempt to improve pastures they often did so at the wrong time and burnt the grass-seeds as well. Over-stocking after good rains quickly obliterated the tender new growth and allowed the further invasion of spinifex, a tough prickly grass that is in itself insufficiently nutritious for efficient milk production.

The prime cause of the disaster then, is the old story of the 'hungry' sheep-farmer who, particularly when wool prices are low, runs as many sheep as possible on unimproved pastures with disastrous consequences to his stock and himself. The euros, typically animals of the tough spinifex lands, could thrive on the poorer plants that were invading the stations. They increased, too, with the artificial improvement of the water supply, and so this aggravated the situation further.

Suijdendorp, an official of the Western Australian Agricultural Department, produced a scheme that provides great hope for the local sheep-farmers. On Muccan Station, which runs about 14,000 sheep and perhaps 20,000 kangaroos, a dramatic improvement in both pastures and stock, including wool production, was made by keeping sheep off burnt pastures until the new grass had itself dropped seed. After the seed fell, the pastures were heavily stocked. The seed was then trampled into the earth before it was blown away, or eaten by birds and insects. Apparently nobody in this area had realised before that if sheep are allowed to eat almost every scrap of seeding grass, not even the most earnest prayers will produce a lush grassy landscape after the next season's rains.

As the farmers ruin the land, and allow the overflow of coarse spinifex, the euro, traditionally a 'rough country' animal, rejoices. The euro is marvellously adapted for life in dry, relatively waterless areas. Ealey proved that it can survive for several months without drinking, provided that it can shelter from the heat of the sun in caves and behind rocks. With the heat at 115 degrees Fahrenheit the euro, like the reptiles of the dry lands, alters its position so that it can remain in the rocky shade at 95 degrees or less. It does not move or feed until the cool of the evening. When it must have water, it scratches up the sand of the dry creek beds and gets it there. In waterless desert between Broome and Marble Bar, Ealey found euros living in comfort wherever there was the kindly shelter of caves.

Another beneficial specialisation is that female euros are practically always pregnant. Almost as soon as the single 'joey' is born, and reaches the nipple in the mother's pouch, the female mates again. However, as long as the pouch young one is attached to the nipple the development of the tiny embryo within the mother is delayed. When the pouch baby stops feeding, the internal foetus begins to grow. So the process is repeated and, in good times, a young euro can be launched into the environment every eight or nine months.

The success of many Australian marsupials in the face of economic competition by sheep and cattle makes us wonder whether these relatively primitive pouched creatures are really 'second class mammals' as is so often supposed. It is true that many marsupials have faded because of the destruction of their special haunts by man, and by economic competition from imported mammals. But the zoologist Storr has pointed out that when even the rodent rats (among the most 'efficient' and 'progressive' of animals) of one country are invaded by rats from a larger land-mass, the home stocks have given way to the invaders. This idea has interesting genetical implications that we need not bother with here.

It has to be admitted by even the most ardent conservationists that the euro must be kept within reasonable numbers. Ealey told us of one station that ran 5,000 sheep and at least 40,000 kangaroos. So far, no humane method of control has been devised. The most efficient means is to poison artificial water-points for a prolonged period (giving the euro time to get thirsty) every several years. Inevitably, by the use of this method, thousands of native birds, too, lose their lives and, periodically, the Perth press is inundated by letters from readers protesting that the euro should be left alone, or its numbers reduced by shooting. Unhappily, neither suggestion is a workable proposition.

Tim told us firmly that Australian sheep-farmers do not like to be termed as such. They prefer to be called 'graziers' or 'pastoralists'. They enjoy a higher social status than their counterparts, the sheep-farmers of the Cotswolds and Scotland, or the sheep-herders of the United States. They are richer, too, and generally speaking, better educated.

The evolution of the grazier is an interesting story. On the heels of the explorers there followed a peripatetic group who herded sheep on the native grasses. These were the convict days, and a free man or a recently freed man (or emancipist, as he was politely called) squatted, or otherwise took up land. So, legally, or illegally, he became a 'squatter' on a 'sheep run'. With increasing affluence there emerged a pleasant, and often by no means uncultivated, set of people who became 'graziers'. The logic is obscure why a dairy farmer should *not* be called a grazier; nor why a pig-farmer be called a pig-farmer and not a snuffier, or some other such term.

The acquisition of a large acreage and an appreciable bank balance led to the evolution of a rural society. The children from the distant sheep-farms came to form a large proportion of the boarders at the Australian equivalent of the English public schools. Admirably, in one respect, but unhappily in another, the matriculant sons and daughters of sheep-farmers generally chose to read for degrees in arts rather than in agricultural science.

As long as they were allowed to retain their large original holdings, sheep-farmers could carry on in a time-honoured and wasteful way. It was, generally speaking, *infra dig* to put even part of one's land under wheat, although more and more intelligent station-owners do so today in times of financial stringency. By and large, however, the appropriate thing to do was, and is, to run sheep, and sheep only. It became a pleasant fiction that with sheep no personal effort is required. Sheep move from paddock to paddock by rotation and, although there are many worries associated with foot rot, blow-flies and the recurrent spectre of drought, it was generally held that to farm in the orthodox sense of the word placed a fellow on the level of a cow-cocky – a dairy farmer. To farm *pigs* (as the cow-cockies and the English do) was the very end!

Nowadays, most of the big properties have been dissected, and two or more of the sons of former owners, or else 'soldier settlers', occupy the more extensive of the former holdings. The best of the present generation are ploughing tactically to repair the erosion caused by their ignorant and greedy fore-runners. Many are becoming knowledgable in the use of superphosphates and the like. They are uninhibitedly planting wheat in order fully to utilise their properties. Gradually, a more learned and responsible class of person is inheriting the land.

14

At Woodstock they told of their modern ghost. Talk of ghosts surprised us for in Australia ghosts are unfashionable; they have no place in society. In European countries the woods abound with headless horsemen. Dogs move unimpeded through bricked up walls, and Prudence, betrayed by a cavalier, walks in Magpie Lane. In Australia, no. If a chap gets himself drowned at a river crossing they plant him, and that is that. Not since the earliest colonial days of superstitious settlers has any flapping white sheet in the half-light given birth to a ghost. No murmuring of voices, no ghostly banging of doors. No leprechauns, no poltergeists. Solemn accounts in English newspapers of the vicar of Little Puddleton-Under-the-Mud exorcising a ghost that has proved troublesome in the village are a source of sheer delight for visitors from Wagga Wagga.

So it was that we were astounded to hear of the Woodstock ghost. And no mean ghost either – but, in fact, the ghost of a huge diesel truck.

Nobody has actually *seen* it, but everybody has heard it. If you live in the silence, with a great empty land all around, sound becomes portentous. Therefore, a diesel engine wracking through the night, changing gears up and down as it labours to the sandy bed of the creek, has people waking from their sleep. Then they follow its progress down over the first hump and then through the long slow grind across the sand.

'What's going across the creek?'

Then the engine beat gives out and there is once again the silence. But in the morning there are no tracks, nothing to show that a stranger has passed. The mystery remains unexplained. At no time has a diesel truck been killed in the area. The C.S.I.R.O. men have pondered long on what natural phenomena would cause echoes that would produce the nocturnal gear-changes.

'I don't believe in ghosts,' says Tim Ealey, 'but if I did, I'd say that it was just some poor bastard who never made the pub!'

There are ever materialists among us who wish to ascribe natural cases to the ghostly phenomena of Woodstock. Such people point out that earthquakes are often accompanied by sounds resembling those made by a heavily laden motor vehicle approaching, and then receding, from the anxious listener. But the earth at Woodstock is as stable as that of Surbiton; and when was there ever an earthquake that did not even shake your bed? Other people have asserted that the Woodstock manifestation is caused by the contracting of sand, and the consequent shifting of the slopes with an accompanying eerie sound. Although there is sand in the river bed, there are no very big dune slopes. The ghost truck *may* be caused by some natural agency but no simple explanation will readily explain it away. We have both lived among the splendidly varied ghosts of England; and so we have become just a tiny bit out of sympathy with this typically Antipodean scepticism concerning the supernatural. We are of the opinion that the ghost truck could perhaps be laid only by a ceremony of exorcism performed by the Archbishop of Perth (who could easily be flown up) or, if he declined to conduct the service, perhaps one by the chairman of directors of General Motors-Holden's.

Although undoubtedly there are no records of proof, it seems perfectly obvious that at some past period in this area a large and noisy diesel truck must have been done away with. We have little doubt that a careful search among the flowering eucalypts and melaleucas of the lonely creek-sides would reveal the body, we mean chassis, very cunningly concealed. Alas, the few white inhabitants there are more concerned with material things.

Tim Ealey guided us to Gallery Hill, an extraordinary granite outcrop some miles along the track to Marble Bar, whose great

Whose boulders are engraved with hundreds of petroglyphs by long-gone generations.

boulders are engraved with hundreds of petroglyphs by long-gone generations of aboriginal artists. Tim said that local aborigines told him that this work was done by the White Owl people who were extinguished long before the 'modern' brown man came into the land. Tim was told by some that bad spirits had made the engravings.

The granite, weathered and butchered by nature, maintains a curious order and delicacy and rises like architecture out of the plain. Rock on rock is incised with totemic figures of goannas, euros, tortoises, and particularly realistic interpretations of the coming into being of life. These men had no iron. Somehow they carved deeply into the tough granite with stone. The carvings appear almost golden in colour for they are hammered into, and beneath, the age-old patina of red brown that covers the boulders, so that they appear with startling clarity in the bright sunlight.

One would imagine that the laborious method of hammering and pecking would inhibit the artist to severe formalism. Instead, the figures display the exultant freedom of a drawing swept in with chalk, and so convey a state of excitement and movement that is both sophisticated and arresting. Each mountain side was an immense art gallery on a broken wall several hundred feet high. We suppose it was natural for us modern Europeans to wonder how many man-hours were involved and, at the same time, ridiculously to feel slightly guilty in so doing. The place had something of the quality of Chartres, but there was no music, only silence as the galleries stood ageless and immobile in the wind and desert air.

We learnt later that a German missionary, Father Worms, had spent a considerable time in the area and published hypothetical conclusions about the vanished artists and their work. On the lowest stratum, the petroglyphs seem to be older than the rest. They are less definite and they depict other things. They represent human figures but these do not bear elaborate coiffures and their distortion employs differing devices. Some of these lower figures are indistinct, and many have later engravings superimposed upon them. Nevertheless, some remain in their original state, and in these Father Worms has seen a similarity to other carvings of Port Hedland and Depuch and has concluded that they belong to an earlier culture that penetrated inland from the coast.

The later culture, responsible for the loftier works, perhaps appeared from the south-eastern deserts and is said to be representative of the Guranara rite which found its way north into the Kimberleys, supposedly in historical times. This rite is connected with Mangula, the sacred woman, and her consort, Djanba, the culture hero. Worms refers to the culminating rite of ceremonial sexual intercourse of groups, a ceremony called Karangara or Guranara, involving the exchange of wives.

If this is true it would be reasonable to suppose that Gallery Hill was still in use for sacred ceremonies up to the time of white penetration. But whether it was, or not, it would be fascinating if one could step back in time and see the dark brown men gathered about its rocks. One can picture them squatting or standing high on the pinnacles, pounding and hammering into the granite, the sweat running down the ochre of their foreheads, grunting in time to the rhythm of the blows, or with voices lifted in an age-old chant. Men of the old stone age, creating a great gallery of art. It is conceivable that while the builders of Chartres were raising their sublime creation to the glory of God, these children of the dawn were engraving their vision of the creation of mankind on a cathedral wrought by the elements from the face of the earth, a vision open to the wide light of the sky, to the singing winds of the desert and the sparse and cooling rain.

These people built no houses, nor temples to their gods. Their gods were heroes of the dream-time in which all creatures were created, and they existed in the sagas and legends of their poetry. It seemed that when they depicted them they did so in the likeness of themselves, or in the likeness of the ancestor-animals of their world. Perhaps we could never describe a landscape as a nomad desert-dweller saw it. We see and recognize the familiar furnishings of a landscape; mountains and rivers, trees and rocks, scrub and plain, hill and gully, and these attributes always exist in varying degrees and proportions. Because of our urban conditioning we feel a certain detachment as we survey or admire, or even stand a little awed, before some view. But for the wild man, mountains may take on the form of giants; and thunder, the voice of outraged deities. Pools and glades may harbour kindly or ill-disposed spiritual ancestors, human or other animal. To the wild man the landscape is endowed with the magic of life. In the time of the dreaming there was the beginning, and in life there is the memory of the dream; in death, the world of the dream. This is the poetry of emergence and re-emergence, a world seen and explained through the eyes of magic.

These people, with their flaked and pointed hammer-stones, and with the heavy blows required to incise granite rock, produced this vigorous and exciting art. That it is situated in a lonely and remote region, where few may look, heightens its air of mystery. Its meaning lost to the minds of the aborigines today, this art will stand for ages as a memorial to a strange cult, and a people of immense imagination. Our last memory of Gallery Hill was the sight of a strange figure etched high upon a great rock that shone golden in the sunlight, the mark of a long lost man made in obedience to the magic of his mind.

The Woodstock pub was built as an overnight halt and drinking house for the itinerant gold mining fraternity in the late nineteenth century. Men in cotton shirts and corduroys met there to buy provisions and to 'blue' their cheques on fiery spirits or *shypoo*, as colonial beer was called. These were troubled times. The early British colonists, here as in other parts of the world, had no scruples about taking up native land, including sacred places. The brown man contended with the white invader. The prospector was interesed only in gold and water, and set down his packs indifferent to the traditional rights of the wild men who knew nothing of gold but to whom water meant life. Brown men were killed. When the solid Woodstock pub was built the bodies of men who asserted their rights to the stream on which it was built were flung in among its foundations.

'In the old days,' a sheep-farmer told us, 'they had a lot of trouble with the blacks.'

Today the landscape rests in peace. The aboriginal descendants mostly live in camps, or work on stations, as they please. The great majority are not pleased to work consistently, and many who appear likely to do so tend periodically to leave their jobs and go 'walkabout' on hunting trips. The aborigine has never tilled the land – he has always been a hunting nomad accustomed to shifting his camp over large distances according to the prevailing supply of game and water. The aborigine is probably as intelligent as any other racial type. Not surprisingly, however, he lacks, in general, the intellectual drive that has carried many negroes and New Zealand Maoris to high education and positions of responsibility. Because he apparently never made gardens, nor even a permanent house, the legend arose that these nomad hunters are an unintelligent, hopelessly primitive people.

'You know what?' a white sheep-farmer once said to one of us in eastern Australia. 'The abo's brain is only half the size of a white man's!'

Only thoroughly stupid persons believe this sort of thing today. We have met aboriginals no less intelligent than many B.A.s of our acquaintance, though perhaps some will say that this is not claiming very much. The complexity of their social organisation is often cited as an indication of their intelligence, but complex, too, is the social organisation of ants, bees, and termites. The proof of aboriginal intelligence is not in their traditional social patterns, but in the conversation of individuals, in their dependability as stockmen, and as black trackers in pursuit of criminals, and in their prowess as hunters in some parts of the country in which a lizard is hard put to stay alive.

It is generally believed, though without proof, that when the British settlers made their first camp at Sydney Cove there were about 300,000 aborigines in Australia. Today there are about 27,000 half-caste and 47,000 full-blood aborigines. The numbers of the latter, after a century and a half of decline, are increasing fast. Recent years have seen the first aborigines graduate from universities by the aid of free scholarships reserved for them. These scholarships were not established by the government, but were made possible by the collection of money for the purpose by the National Union of Australian University Students.

On to Marble Bar. This old mining town has long been famed as the hottest place in Australia. Perhaps few other places sustain such high average temperatures. Marble Bar lies about a hundred miles inland from Woodstock, and the track there is rough and

Aboriginal child. R.D. 61.

The numbers of full-bloods, after a century and a half of decline, are increasing fast.

rocky. This Pilbara country is hard granite, with great shattered boulders and rough-bottomed creeks. The sun belts down on the rock and the reflected heat beats back like a blast furnace. We were now on the first leg of the journey down the Madman's Track with still more than a thousand miles to go to Kalgoorlie. This is the old track that they used to say only a madman would use. A thousand miles of mulga and sandy country, with dry creek beds and plenty of sunshine. Marble Bar, then Nullagine, a tiny township whose gold has all but gone. Then hundreds of miles to Meekathara with very few station homesteads in between.

Outside the town of Marble Bar we pulled off the road, and found The Bar itself. This is a massive slab of red and blue jasper flung like a dam across a precipitous valley. Fingered and tempered by time, the Marble Bar sprawls over the wide dry river

The Boss   Russell Drysdale wa.

A thirsty station boss came into the Ironclad and demanded a beer 'off the ice'.

bed. The town could have no other name. It was relatively cool, only 98 degrees, when we passed through, but we made for the Ironclad Hotel, nevertheless. This is the only pub left in the town. The settlement is surrounded by granite hills; it drowses in the bottom of a cauldron.

They told us their favourite story. It concerned the man from Marble Bar who went to hell and immediately called for an overcoat. And another story, of the days before refrigeration. A thirsty station boss came into the Ironclad and demanded of the barmaid a beer 'off the ice'.

He was served. He tasted it, and barked: 'I said, off the ice!'

She said: 'You've got it, Mate. Six hundred miles off the ice!'

In the pub it was cool, and the barman told us that the track had been newly graded and was good going all the way south. Outside, the wide street looked white in the heat and a group of aborigines sat listlessly in the shade of the awning, brushing lazily at flies, and not always bothering to do that. A large half-caste gentleman came in and bought six bottles of port. He took the top off one and poured himself a glassful. He knocked this back in one hit. Then he gathered up his *plonk* and strode out through the door.

At one end of the bar there was taking place one of those never-ending arguments about which the participants were too tired or drunk to care very much, but which they kept going as a matter of form than because of any convictions in the matter. The drone of flies and the whirring of an ineffectual electric fan supplied a background of subdued noise, against which the conversation at the end of the bar rose and fell like waves. We drank the cold beer gratefully and in silence, for coming in out of the glare it was pleasant to fall into a kind of trance. We remembered to buy rum for the camp, for it gets chilly at night in the mulga. After a last beer we wandered back to the truck and headed her out of town.

The barman was right. The Madman's Track, the old enemy, is no track, but a well formed-up road on which we could wallop along at fifty miles an hour. The road runs over rough hills and down into the bottoms of valleys and ravines. There is little growth apart from a few trees, most of which grow along the dry creek beds. The evening brought relief from the heat. Once more the sky became a rich dark blue that turned in the west to gold.

Topping a rise we saw the road winding down to a creek in the valley and below, beside the sandy bed with a fire going, we saw that Dom (who had gone ahead, after dropping Don Farner at an airstrip) had made camp.

Young Tim pulled the truck over to the camp and hauled out a ·303 and walked down the valley in the hope of bagging a 'roo for meat. But the light was fading, and though he got in a couple of shots, it was too dark to shoot accurately at long range. The hills about us looked like a landscape from the moon. They were bald hills, made up of shaley, broken stone, between which clumps of spinifex grew. These hills rose steeply all around, and the tops, where the last light caught them, glowed a red that quickly faded to russet brown. It was extremely quiet. Our voices echoed, and the crackle of the fire sounded unusually loud. We dined on packaged soup, some tinned meat and bread, and plenty of sweet black tea.

We built the fire up that night for we thought it would get chilly in the hours before dawn. It did, too, but as soon as the morning sun struck down, the earth warmed quickly and there was promise of another hot day. The morning light on the hills was incredibly beautiful for the slopes became rose-red, and the spinifex looked like spun gold. High on the slopes a 'roo paused to look down upon us, his brisket a sharp white in contrast to the ochre gloss of the rest of him. For a minute he stood there without moving, the ancient inhabitant gazing curiously at the newcomers. Then he turned about and loped unhurriedly over the brow of the hill where, for a brief moment, he stood once more silhouetted against the sunlight, a symbol of a lonely world.

We drove on in convoy, missing the presence of Ivan Carnaby and Don Farner who always added amusement to the campfire talk at night. We were now down to four. We felt rather like the ten little nigger boys, for we were to lose Dom at Kalgoorlie, when he would go west to Perth and home. The hills and valleys continued until we reached the tiny town of Nullagine. Here was a handful of houses, and the inevitable pub. This goes under the original name of the Conglomerate Hotel.

We paused here. We talked to Mrs Howard, who runs the pub. She has a small son about ten years old, but his grave and self-possessed manner gave him an appearance much in excess of his years. He had with him a pet blue-winged kookaburra, a bird as grave as he, and whose plumage was brilliantly coloured. We spent a delightful hour and listened to stories of the old days when the gold was good. Then we topped up the water-tanks, and the front-slung water bags, for we had a long dry run ahead of us.

We said farewell and drove out across the creek beneath the tall gums. Dom took the lead in the smaller Land Rover and we followed at a distance to avoid his dust. The going was remarkably good. The land became less hilly and at length we found ourselves in the flat mulga country. We camped near a wide, sandy creek that night with plenty of firewood. We saw no 'roos and we were without fresh meat. One of us rolled a damper and set it on the fire for a late snack. But we all fell soundly asleep and we remembered it only in the morning. It had cooked slowly and beautifully, for it was an even charcoal right through.

It requires vigilance as well as experience to achieve a good damper. Not so, however, in the cooking of the johnny-cake, the second great standby of the bushman. The johnny-cake must be almost the simplest form of cooking, apart from boiling an egg. All you do is take some flour and water and mix them together into a paste. This is worked into a thin, stiff, saucer-shaped wafer which must be dropped flat on the glowing embers of a raked over or dying fire. When the dough is cooked crisp you have a johnny-cake. (Some bush cooks mix a bit of fat with the flour.)

The making of a good damper is a complicated and somewhat mystical operation. You take flour and water as before. Carefully you make a big mound of the flour, and in its centre you scoop a deep depression. Into this crater you pour enough water to form a small lake. Now you work the edges of the lake inwards until you have a big lump of firm, damp dough. This should be kneaded so that air will be mechanically incorporated. This is a highly important part of the process. The amount of kneading is part of the *mystique* of damper making. Next, you shape the lump of aerated dough into a circular slab, not more than three inches thick. The degree of thickness is quite enormously important.

Now is the time to rake the burning branches off the fire until only a bed of fiery embers remains. A deep depression is scooped in the glowing charcoal, and into this the damper is dropped flat. Many bushmen allow the damper to remain like this for a few minutes; it 'lets the outside get used to the heat', they say. This is part of the *mystique* of damper making. Finally, clean smouldering coals are raked inwards and the damper is now covered. It is thus submerged in a simple 'oven' of exceedingly hot embers.

After a suitable period (varying according to the size of the damper) some of the top embers are scraped away so that the damper can be tested with the point of a knife. This can be done more than once. At length, it sounds hollowish to the tap. Now it is golden brown in colour, and may be reverently disinterred. It smells like fresh heaven, and is ready for eating.

We continued to take specimens, hunting in the early mornings and in the cool evenings, or occasionally in the heat wherever we happened to pull in during the day. In this manner we worked our way south. To the west, the land stretched some hundreds of miles to the coast, somewhere north of Carnarvon. To the east, we had nothing but the Great Central Desert that sprawls for a thousand miles to Alice Springs. We ran south along this desert fringe. That does not mean that to the west was mulga and good country, and to the east nothing but sand. The land that ran to the west certainly is relatively harsh and arid, with sparsely settled grazing in the better portions. Nevertheless, the watercourses run during the rains, and, in many places, wells assure water for stock. The Central Desert does not fit the customary conception of undulating sand on which nothing grows. This desert is made of stable dunes several hundred yards apart that stretch in an east-west direction for hundreds of miles. But they would not always be made out by the casual eye for they are lightly covered by a variety of grasses, desert acacia, much mulga and desert oak or, sometimes, clumps of ghost gums that point to the presence of occasional watercourses that periodically fill with the rains.

It is pitiless country in the dry season, but the soil is good. As we ran south we saw the country change with dramatic emphasis due to the effects of rain. The whole surface of the ground was now carpeted by flowers; hundreds of square miles of flowers. The pink parakeelia, purple moola-moola, and many varieties of ever-lastings; acre after acre. At night we camped in an enchanted land; the landscape, with its graceful forms of stunted acacia and limitless expanses of flowers, looked in a curious way like an enormous Japanese garden. Dampier admired this western flora in the 17th century. 'Most of the Trees and Shrubs had at this time either Blossoms or Berries on them. The Blossoms of the different sort of Trees were of several Colours, as Red, White, Yellow, etc. but mostly Blue: and these generally smelt very sweet and fragrant, as did some also of the rest. There were also beside some Plants, Herbs and tall Flowers, some very small Flowers, growing on the Ground, that were sweet and beautiful, and for the most part unlike any I had seen elsewhere.' This desiccated soil holds within itself the seeds and nourishment to produce a cornucopia of growth. It is not sterile sand. All it needs is water.

Sometimes the country would end in a gentle escarpment,

breaking away in a tumble of rocks to give us a long view across the land. But for much of the way the road just bored on through the mulga. Then, sometimes, we would run into a patch of open country that was stony and sparse without the benefit of rain. Or we would come to big creeks, with large river gums following their courses.

It was at one such watercourse, flowing coastwards eventually to join one of the big rivers of the western watershed, that we pulled up to have a spell and a drink from the water bag. Great eucalypts stretched overhead, and the down-stream was thickly overgrown with tea-tree scrub.

Attracted by the twitter of birds we more or less automatically pushed along the bank. Sharply we came on a clear space in the dry bed of the stream and found there a small, muddied hole that still contained a little water. A cloud of birds flew up. This was one of the few pools remaining after the previous rains and it was the sole watering place in our camp area. We set up the movie camera in the dense growth. It was worth so doing.

The first birds in were a pair of pigeons, their bronze wings flashing in the sun. Then came budgerygahs, brilliant green and yellow. Pink galahs, rainbow-coloured bee-eaters, honey-eaters, crested pigeons and zebra finches came flooding in. A spotted bower-bird hopped along a log and arrogantly surveyed the lesser men about him. Then they all flew off suddenly. We made little note of this because we imagined that the noise and movement of spool-changing had been disruptive. Then we saw what the trouble was. Striding slowly out of the opposite thicket, with forked tongue flickering, came a magnificent goanna of sinister beauty. He was close to six feet long and resplendent in bright yellow and black. Without hesitation he came to the edge of the pool.

The goannas are one of the few groups of reptiles with a forked tongue. When our black-and-yellow beauty flicked his dark tongue repeatedly out and in again, he was testing the air. Goannas, like snakes, have a highly functional organ of Jacobson which consists of twin sacs in the roof of the mouth. These are supplied by branches of the nerves of smell that lead up to the brain. That flickering double-barrelled tongue was carrying particles of scent from the surrounding air into the auxiliary smell-organ in the roof of its mouth. We lay still. There was no breeze. So far, the big lizard had not seen us, nor had he smelled us through his nostrils nor sensed our hidden presence by means of his tongue and through the roof of his mouth. He advanced, flopped luxuriously into the puddle, and lay there.

The name goanna is a corruption of iguana, a family of big and unrelated lizards of the Americas, Fiji and Madagascar. Often, the term is said to have been brought in by prospectors from California, but this is not true because it was in common usage before the discovery of gold. The same was said of the introduction of the American name opossum for the phalangers, but, when we look at Phillip's *Voyage to Botany Bay* and some of the other foundation books, we see that the name opossum was used in Australia half a century before the inrush of the gold-seekers.

Goannas are so called only in Australia, where more kinds live than anywhere else. They occur also in Africa and Asia. The biggest living goanna, the Komodo dragon of Indonesia, is sometimes about fifteen feet in length. The biggest Australian species is the perenti of Central Australia, which grows to eight feet long. Half a million years ago, a twenty-foot goanna, *Megalania*, roamed Australia at the same time as a ten-foot kangaroo, an emu-like bird of similar height, and *Diprotodon*, a wombat-like creature about as big as an extremely large ox.

Suddenly, the big goanna's tongue began to flicker rapidly. He looked suspiciously in our direction. Slowly he raised his bulk from the muddy water. Unhurriedly he made off in the direction from which he had come. And quickly his place was taken by finches, pigeons and parrots. Again the spotted bower-bird, with lilac crest calm and flat, jumped along the log.

These days we dined well, for there was plenty of meat, including emus. Once, at a pleasant camp on the banks of a timbered creek that still held large pools of clear water, Tim shot a young hen emu that turned Dom Serventy's bigger scales at seventy pounds. At a later camp we were cooking steaks from its heavily muscled legs, and lounging about the fire with some rum, when a truck pulled up. Out jumped a pleasant young station owner. He had a noggin with us. He told us that his property was about ten miles further down the road. Time passed, and we invited him to stay and eat with us. He hesitated. Then he heard that we were about to eat emu.

'Jesus!' he said.

We gave him polite attention.

'You can't eat that stuff!' he cried, 'it's bloody muck. My blackfellas eat it. Lord, you can smell it on 'em for days after. I just couldn't come at it, thanks all the same.'

Nor would he. As he downed another large rum he watched us, fascinated. After a while he hauled himself to his feet. He invited us all to call in for lunch tomorrow at the homestead when, he said, he'd see that we got some *real* tucker.

He was an exceedingly pleasant chap but, like a lot of country people today, just could not accept the thought of eating emu. In the pioneering days bush tucker of necessity formed the main diet in many places and, as recently as a little before the turn of the century, kangaroo chops and 'roo-tail soup figured on the menus of city hotels. With increased production of cheap mutton and beef, bush foods disappeared from 'good' tables.

One old country dish, and a very good one too, was galah pie. But most people today have never heard of it, let alone tasted it. As a result the great majority have come to regard the eating of 'roo or other bush tucker as putting oneself on the subsistence level of tribal aborigines. This is all to the good. It means that wild ducks are almost the only animals that Australians shoot for food, although in the settled areas Italian migrants have begun to put themselves on the wrong side of the law by eating willy wagtails, jacky winters, kookaburras ('ha ha pigeons') and, in fact, almost everything in feathers.

Because we could not hang our emu meat and had to eat it comparatively fresh, we cut the steaks thin and fried them in the pan. They tasted like beef steaks. Properly cooked, almost any animal makes a good dish. Even the goannas, or bung-arrows, as the Western Australians call them, can be made into reasonable food. On Cape York Peninsula one of us was fascinated to see white stockmen almost invariably confine their diet to salt beef, damper and bush pickles. In the aboriginal camps nearby the menu consisted of barramundi speared in the rivers, wild sucking pig, geese and ducks, scrub turkey and squatter pigeon. One wondered who really were the savages – the white or the black? Bush pickles, according to the old recipe, are made by stirring a bottle of Worcester sauce into a large tin of plum jam. This can be varied to suit individual tastes.

The emu was eaten from the earliest days of colonial settlement. Captain John Hunter, the Scot who succeeded Phillip in 1795 to become the second governor of New South Wales, left record of its edibility. Those days the bird was generally called either a cassowary or an ostrich in confusion with birds of the East Indies and Africa respectively. 'The flesh of this bird,' wrote Hunter of the emu, 'although coarse, was thought by us delicious meat; it had much the appearance, when raw, of neck-beef; a party of five, myself included, dined on a side-bone of it most scrumptuously . . .'

It could be said, of course, that the reduced state of the infant colony sharpened Hunter's appreciation of emu flesh. 'The pot or spit received every thing which we could catch or kill, and the common crow was relished here as well as the barn-door fowl is in England.'

A mature emu may weigh as much as 120 pounds and a kick from its powerful legs can disembowel a dog. After the female lays her eight or ten dark green, twenty-ounce eggs, the male takes over. He broods and guards them for about two months. The emu is essentially vegetarian. It eats mostly fruits, berries and grasses, although it also likes caterpillars. It would seem, then, that here is an animal that could never become a pest. Yet, mobs of them sometimes break into ripening wheat fields, devouring much grain, but trampling and destroying more than they eat.

And so the usual situation arose: farmers bawling for the blood of an attractive animal, and harassed protectionists trying to discover a means by which both crops and emu could be saved. Dom, as ardent a conservationist as anyone, told us that he has no doubt that the farmers had a grievance, however sympathetic one might feel towards the apparently harmless bird which appears as the left supporter on the national emblem.

The problem was reduced by the removal of the emu from the protected list north of a certain latitude, and the payment by local boards of a shilling, or sometimes half-a-crown, per head or beak. The government rabbit-proof fences that stretch hundreds of miles across the land helped to protect the wheat fields. During the droughts, mass movements of emus were halted by these fences and their skeletons bleached in hundreds along the wires.

'The farmers on the south side of the fence are jubilant,' one Vermin Inspector reported during a particularly severe drought some years ago.

A grotesque chapter in the story began in the summer of 1932 when what is ironically called the Emu War broke out. A mass invasion of emus pushed into the north-eastern wheat belt and, in those depression years, the Commonwealth government allowed itself to be persuaded to supply a unit of machine-gunners in an attempt at mass-destruction. It is pleasing to recall that the Australian army now suffered one of its rare defeats. Perhaps the army was not actually defeated; one supposes, really, that the honours were about even. The emu 'enemy' behaved like some of our allies in Greece, the Malayan Peninsula and New Guinea. They declined to stand and fight.

As the years passed, the big birds were checked in the wheat belt by the bounty, or by the distribution of free ammunition to farmers. By neither method is the emu likely to be extinguished. It still breeds within thirty miles of the state capital. We never saw them in great numbers but Dom says that hordes of them still periodically converge on the wheat farms from the dry areas beyond.

We accepted the young station man's invitation to lunch the next day. We found his house set back from the road amidst tall trees and green lawns, a charming oasis scores of miles from anywhere. His wife fed us as though we were starving schoolboys. They plied us, too, with great mugs of cold beer. The repast was, in fact, better than rum and emu.

Meekatharra, at the end of the railway, and some hundreds of miles north-east of Perth, was a bustling centre after the solitude of the open spaces. There was mail at the post-office. We had our usual session, silently drinking in a cool bush bar as we read and re-read letters from Hampstead and Sydney, Yale, Tanganyika, Oxford and Charterhouse Square. They made us seem remote in our isolation; and we devoured all the small gossip and related bits to each other. We rarely saw newspapers, and when we did they were long out of date. While on the track we became used to a mode of life in which news was never expected, nor did we much want it. Yet when we reached any centre our urban instincts were revived and we found ourselves hungry for newsprint.

Next, Wiluna, where the mineral has cut out, and where half the standing buildings lack occupants. We passed a broad, shallow sheet of water. In this lake, over the years, the savages – white, not pigmented – had dumped slag from a nearby mine. Yet here, without doubt, was an ill-wind that had done some good, for large numbers of graceful white-headed stilts, and stumpy little red-kneed dotterels were using the piles of debris as island nest-sites that protected them from dingoes, imported European foxes and feral cats. There were avocets, too, and Pacific herons, marsh terns, and grey teal. These beautiful birds contentedly graced the outskirts of a once populous town, an area that had echoed to the sound of hundreds of gold-seekers. Now it is just another small isolated centre serving the pastoral industry in a hungry country where the population is sparse and properties far and wide apart. Today the railway to Wiluna is abandoned and supplies are brought in by road from the Meekatharra rail-head. We were now at the southern terminus of the Canning Stock Route, the thousand-mile trail from the Kimberleys that Canning, accompanied by Rob Moody, had pioneered in the early years of the century.

Nowadays, the old Canning Track across the Central Desert is seldom used, and its wells and tanks are falling into disrepair. Only small parties of desert aborigines make use of them, and the chant of the rainmaker has displaced the crack of stockwhips and the bellowing of cattle.

South of Wiluna the road took us into breakaway country, winding down through huge boulders. We came to a tiny pub, miles from anywhere. This is the Kathleen Valley Hotel. Actually, it is the homestead of a property. The owners, the good Mr Moriarty and his wife, run the pub as a side-line. We stopped at this remote place and were welcomed. This is a real old-time pub with a tiny bar opening into a parlour that is simply furnished and has aboriginal relics hanging on its walls. The talk turned to animals and Dom made enquiries whether Mrs Moriarty, who was interested in wild things, had noticed a particular and local species of quail-thrush in which he was interested. Mrs Moriarty was not sure, and went to fetch a book on the subject. Her reference, we were delighted to see, turned out to be The Word, in short, Serventy and Whittell's *Birds of Western Australia*.

The question now was whether the author, or the owner, should buy the next beer for all hands. We had made camp a few miles away and Mrs Moriarty invited us back for the evening to meet her husband who was at the moment out on the sheep run. We spent the evening drinking, and talking of animals and aboriginal customs. They told us of the 'pet' colony of honey-ants to which they took visitors. Next day Tom Moriarty took us to a part of his property where he said we could obtain the quail-thrush and see the bowers of spotted bower-birds.

We were now a mere two hundred miles north of Kalgoorlie. We came to the small town of Leonora in the clear evening light. We decided to eat in a café, and then push on for another fifty miles before making camp. We ate steak and eggs and drank mugs of tea. Then we called at the pub to pick up some rum for the evening campfires. Tonight would be Dom's last camp, for next day we would reach Kalgoorlie. Two of us, and Tim Drysdale,

At a distance the few buildings have a solid appearance, but when we reached them ...

would then start the long run over the Nullarbor Plain to the Maralinga bomb-range where we had some more work to do. Dom would drive west along the bitumen to Perth. Our camp that night was spectacular. The ground was carpeted by everlastings, and we built a great fire of mulga that illuminated the scene so well that we were able to take photographs. We lay in our swags talking about the past weeks, about the tracks covered, the places seen, and the people whom we had met.

Next morning we shaved and dug out reasonably clean clothes. We brushed up the vehicles, too, for that day we would strike the first city we had seen for months. We ran through what remains of the old boom town of Menzies. At a distance the few buildings have a solid appearance, but when we reached them we saw that some were gutted, with sagging verandah posts. Great holes showed in the walls of others. The skeletons of old trucks and cars lay about. The small pub functions also as a store. There is little to show that fortunes were made on its fields.

That afternoon we saw smoke on the horizon, and soon we were on the outskirts of the city. Untidy outskirts, a vista of old poppet heads, and the discarded material of worked-out mines; a scarred and battered landscape. The great Kalgoorlie mines of today are in the town of Boulder a mile or two south of the city proper, and their slag heaps stand up like hills from the flat land. We went to a large old-fashioned hotel and booked ourselves in for the night. We headed straight for the bathrooms and had our first real shower since leaving Woodstock a thousand miles ago. Dressed in crumpled, but passably clean, shirts and ties we had the most curious experience of a waiter in a white jacket bringing us drinks. We read our mail. After months of living in swags in lonely places it was odd to see crowds on the streets. There were strange things like neon lights, cinemas, milk bars and rows of solid suburban houses. Hall's Creek seemed like a place in a dream and the shrill fruit-bats of Geikie Gorge utter fantasy. Yet just beyond the fringes of this city the loneliness begins again. It is 375 miles to neighbouring Perth in the west, and to the east stretches the Nullarbor Plain and the great Victoria Desert. South runs the road to Norseman and the long way across the lower Nullarbor to the South Australian border.

This inland city, landlocked by thin eucalyptus forest, is a curious phenomenon. Its water supply comes in huge pipes pumped all the way from Perth to keep alive a city in an arid land. And there is still gold to mine. But one day, when there is no gold any more, what will happen? Coolgardie, thirty miles away, was once a bustling and thriving town of rich strikes, but there is little there now. In the main street of Coolgardie many large and imposing buildings stand isolated, their neighbours reduced to heaps of rubble, the bones of former banks and business houses. Lying among the rubbish are broken columns, and chipped and shattered pediments, that are all that remain of the pride of former times. But though its glory has departed, Coolgardie remains as a small township in which people dwell. Kanowna, just fifteen miles east of Kalgoorlie, is another matter.

Kanowna is a great mausoleum of blonde and waving grass. There are few trees. This is the graveyard of a city. And it is complete with headstones, for the authorities in nearby Kalgoorlie have erected signposts so that the visitors may read the story of the town. Standing like scarecrows in a paddock, they bear the names of former streets. Here was once the Town Hall where celebration balls were held. Here was the police station, and there the site of the leading hotel whose clientele toasted one another in champagne in great and wealthy days gone by. When we passed there was just one ruin left, the decaying brick walls of what was once a popular pub. The roof has fallen in and the cellar is a gaping hole, but there linger traces in the flaking plaster of an exuberant rococo decor. On a rise a half a mile away is a small cottage made of slabs of corrugated iron. It is set near a clump of trees. In the still of the late afternoon a wisp of smoke drifted from the cottage chimney. This is the home of the last inhabitant of Kanowna, a pensioner who is too old to work, and too old to wish to leave. As long as the cottage and the memories remain, still lives Kanowna.

Wiluna, Menzies, Coolgardie and Kanowna. And there are other towns, too, whose poppet heads and stampers once worked overtime, whose crowded bars and dusty streets rang with the noisy celebrations of new strikes. Once the country seemed to be made of gold, and the faith of its people in the permanence of its wealth was reflected in the substance of the buildings they created. They built with bricks, stone and mortar. But even those substantial things have fallen prey to time and a curious cannibalism. As one town died, other settlements arose, and so old buildings were salvaged for the new. Roofing here, timber there, until only shells remain. Itinerant populations that moved about the land, building and re-building. Of them all, only the city of Kalgoorlie retains an air of permanence.

We spent that evening yarning in the comfort of armchairs. Dom would leave for Perth at first light and would be gone when the rest of us awoke. The others would stock up with fresh stores and set out along the road to Norseman for the long haul over the Nullarbor. Young Tim got the big Land Rover serviced and refuelled, and our tanks and bags were filled with fresh water. Some of us slept a little uncomfortably. We had grown used to sleeping in swags on the ground and the confines of a hotel room seemed rather hot and stuffy.

15

The run to Norseman was a pleasure trip, for the road was sealed with bitumen. We saw wildflowers that we had not encountered before. It was already evening when we pulled into the pub at Norseman. This is a typically straggling and dreary township, and we decided to push straight on for another twenty or thirty miles to make a camp in the bush. We knew that some miles out of Norseman the country would open out, and the scrub would disappear as we began to cross the scorching Nullarbor Plain. The next settlement would be Madura, roughly three hundred and fifty miles to the east.

Some miles out we were stopped by a car heading towards the town. It contained a man and his wife who were motoring through from Adelaide to Perth. They were worried. They had encountered a woman walking in the direction of Madura. She carried, they said, nothing but a string bag with a few skimpy belongings. She had told them that she was walking east across the desert and she had refused to heed their urgent warning that there was no water, or anything else for that matter, for hundreds of miles. The couple had decided that they should inform the Norseman police.

The lady had seemed so determined to risk the desert that, they believed, she might take to the bush if she saw a police car, so we agreed to stop and try and persuade her to wait with us until the police arrived.

Some miles further out we came across the woman standing by the roadside. She was in her late twenties and dressed in a thin cotton frock, a light coat and cheap shoes. Her string bag was stuffed with paper-wrapped parcels. She did not approach the vehicle but stood silently watching us. We talked to her, and explained that if she went on walking that way she could easily perish, for there was no water ahead. She was English, and repeated to us that she wanted to get to Adelaide. We explained patiently that Adelaide was nearly eighteen hundred miles from where she stood. The police did not come so we decided to take her back. She refused. At length we persuaded her to get into the vehicle and we headed her back towards Norseman.

We did not want to take her forward with us for two reasons. A strange woman in our sort of camp would be a nuisance, especially as we would be a considerable time on the road engaged in collecting work. Also, we had to work at the bomb-range at Maralinga, and we could not take an 'unscreened' passenger there.

At Norseman the lady further let us know that she was absolutely without funds and, above all, had no wish for contact with the police force. It was now dark, and cold. Reluctantly, we now agreed to give her a lift to Madura where she could stop in civilised surroundings and then try to pick up a ride on another vehicle going east. A few miles out of town we met the police sergeant and a constable returning after their search for her.

We had a headlight conference in which we attempted once more to persuade her to return with the police to Norseman. She refused, saying positively that, as she had no money with which to pay for board and lodging, the sergeant would be obliged to lock her up on a charge of vagrancy. The sergeant agreed. This was an extraordinary conference in the dark of the long Nullarbor road. We ended it by saying that we would take her forward to Madura. The sergeant was obviously relieved to have her off his hands. He read her a brief lecture on the virtues of work, and the dangers of the waterless plain. Then we departed to make camp in the bush.

It was cold, and we fixed up the front seat of the Land Rover for our strange guest. She did not approach the campfire, nor would she eat. We were up at dawn and soon on our way. The lady and we took little notice of each other. We pulled up here and there in the course of our work. By evening she grew hungry enough to be persuaded to share our meal of steak. She sat with us at the fireside but she did not volunteer her name nor gave much account of herself beyond odd, garbled bits of information that were often highly suspect and once directly contradictory.

Soon we got used to our passenger and went about our job as though she hardly existed.

In this area we saw dozens of mountain devils, a small and curious lizard that looks a little like a spiny miniature dinosaur. It is only about six inches long, and its fearsome appearance is misleading for it is utterly harmless, soft bodied, and equipped with a tiny degenerate mouth capable of dealing with nothing tougher than small black ants.

The road runs past Belladonia Station homestead. The granddaughter of the founder of the station, Mrs Crocker, still lives there and Dom had told us to call in. The homestead is situated on the saltbush plain, and nearby are gigantic granite boulders and the remains of a long dried lake. Here the fossil bones of big mammals have been found. The house itself is built from blocks of limestone of Miocene age, and in the walls are embedded fossil shells and other sea creatures of the period. Mrs Crocker. like so many people of the bush, has a keen interest in the animals around her and she has made beautiful little paintings of the lizards, butterflies, birds and strangely marked spiders of the surrounding plains. These are exquisitely drawn and her feeling for arrangement and colour had made them not merely faithful representations but small works of art.

At a camp between Cocklebiddy and Madura we accidentally made a contribution to the next edition of The Word. We saw a chough. The chough is a conspicuous black bird, not quite as big as a crow, with an unmistakable white 'window pane' in each wing. Familiar from childhood with flocks of this bird in eastern Australia we idly looked it up in the Good Book. It was not there. Then we realised this was one of the species that is normally barred from Western Australia by the faunal barrier of the treeless Nullarbor. But here was a *chough* in Western Australia! Possibly it was merely a single storm-blown straggler, but we must send old Dominic Serventy a signal from the next telegraph station along the track.

Madura came next. Madura is not a town, but merely a roadside pub with sleeping cabins, a bar and a petrol pump or two. It lies at the foot of the escarpment of the Nullarbor Plain. Here the great high plain falls sharply to a secondary plain that runs for some miles to the cliffs of the Great Bight where the Southern Ocean rolls in from the Antarctic. We were now emphatically in the temperate zone. The road winds down the limestone for a mile or two and then reaches up a short rise to the pub. From the enclosed verandah of the pub you can look out across the treeless plain until the horizon is lost in haze.

We talked in the little bar with the pub-keeper, and got information about the next part of the track. The pub-keeper said he would look after the lady. So we gave her an envelope (with a fiver in it) and said that perhaps she would like to wait here until she got a lift with somebody else who would be going eastward. The lady received the envelope and information with rare bad grace. We refuelled and started off towards Eucla, another hundred miles away.

A little beyond the pub we passed the lady sitting on the track, patiently awaiting another traveller.

It was much later, in Adelaide, that we learned something of the probable reason for her presence, and her antipathy towards the local constabulary. Perth traditionally had a relatively sophisticated system of tolerated 'houses'. These were not licensed by the government, as certain visiting sports scribblers have averred. Nevertheless, as long as the ladies kept off the streets, and maintained good order in their establishments, they and these were left to their own business. The system seems to have worked well for many years. Then, a number of years after the expropriation of the property of an interned German national, the government found itself in the embarrassing situation of being the virtual owner of the local red light district.

There was a great deal of argument. Shrewd points were scored both for and (by the churches) against the continuance of the wicked establishments of Rowe Street. The government decided that it could hardly continue as the proprietor of a string of bordellos however virtuously, so to speak, they were conducted. So the ladies were issued with an ultimatum. They must address themselves to more reputable pursuits, or leave the state. Soliciting is not tolerated in Perth, so a stream of indignant ladies left for the east by liner, transcontinental train and by jet. Those who lingered were forced to work by other means, or to steal, or join zoological collecting parties.

The Nullarbor Plain stretches between four and five hundred

miles from east to west, and from a hundred and fifty to two hundred miles northward from the Southern Ocean. It is a relatively recent formation. From the Eocene onwards, huge areas of southern Australia became depressed and were over-run by the sea. By Miocene times, a mere 30 million years ago, the sea covered an area about 300 miles long. On this sea floor coral reefs appeared. Later, the ocean floor arose again, and became the land on which we were now camped. Nobody is quite sure where was the northern edge of this Miocene sea because these former shores were covered by the free-drifting sands of the great inland desert. The astonishing abundance of fossil shells that can be found almost anywhere, as well as the remains of reef-building corals, seem to make it certain that the southern oceans were warmer than they were during the preceding epochs, and much warmer, moreover, than they are now. No such exuberance of marine life exists off the southern Australian coastline today. These Miocene rocks are about 900 feet thick on the present coastline. Here they overlie rocks laid down in Cretaceous seas. A little inland, at the railway, the rocks are about 500 feet thick. Nobody is yet quite sure precisely when the area became dry land. Much of the Nullarbor was lifted again in the Pliocene, about 12 million years ago, but the sea was probably still washing over parts of it at a date much closer to us today.

We drove over a flat treeless plain. The thin covering of topsoil supports chiefly saltbush and bluebush. Once we saw a thin, dead

It was the only tree that we could see and, sure enough, a hawk had made it her home.

and naked tree-trunk arising alone out of the plain. It was the only tree for as far as we could see and, sure enough, a hawk had made it her home. Later we were to see the nests of hawks and crows built starkly among the insulators, every now and then on telegraph poles along the Transcontinental Railway Line. Lacking trees, these birds build their bulky stick nests on the next best thing available.

There are no watercourses here, for the light rainfalls percolate straight down through the porous limestone. In numerous places the action of water has dissolved away the soft rocks beneath the plain, so there exist vast caverns, some of which hold underground lakes. Some of these stygian waters have been explored by small boat. Once or twice we stopped at blow-holes. Many such open out on to bare limestone. Through these holes the air about us was sucked in at a rate that produced a sound like a roaring blow-lamp. We gathered handfuls of twigs and offered them above the funnel-like holes. Instantly the debris was sucked from our grasp into uncharted chasms below.

Between Eyre in the west, and Eucla in the east, there is a narrow coastal plain bounded by a continuous cliff that falls away about 250 feet to the edge of the Southern Ocean. This escarpment runs right around the Great Bight. Some geologists believe that its regularity is caused by a vast fault, not by the action of the sea. About one hundred miles inland runs the Transcontinental Railway. We stopped at one part of the line where the rails stretched unbendingly over the former sea bed for 330 miles, the longest straight run of rails laid by man. North of the railway continues the plain, in places up to fifty miles, where the saltbush and limestone give way to the stable dunes of the Central Desert. At odd places along the coast we saw the wind whip across the bare 'recent' dunes, lifting feathers of fine white sand into the air like smoke. The southern edge of the plain carries a growth of stunted trees, mallee and false sandalwood mostly, and in some places this growth is thick.

There is no township at Eucla. At what is left of the old station homestead there is a small store where you can get tinned food and petrol. The stone buildings of the original homestead are partly engulfed by the coastal dunes. They have long since been abandoned to the relentless movement of the sands. From the top of the nearest dune we saw a great sea of coastal sand, ripple marked, and pluming in the wind. This was a place of complete desolation. Then the road abruptly turns inland to the north, and the vehicle climbed the escarpment to the main plain above. From there we saw back to the west along the coastal plain. To the south stretched the cold blue expanse of the Southern Ocean that ends on the ice-cliffs of the Antarctic Continent.

The south wind blew strong and bit shrewdly; we dug sweaters out of our swags. After months in the tropical north this place chilled. The Nullarbor always seems to be cold at night. It may be shimmering hot by day, but the wind springs up suddenly with the sunset and whistles through the sandalwood. The stunted scrub was thick along the top of the escarpment and we pulled into a small clearing to cook and camp. Soon we had going a great fire of mallee roots, and a large billy full of soup, with rum on the side to keep us warm. The night sky became overcast but it did not rain. That night we slept in our swags with extra blankets. We pulled tarpaulins over our Matildas and ourselves to keep out the nipping and eager air.

The origin of the use of the name Matilda for a man's swag is unknown. The popularity of the song concerning the gentleman – one of thousands – who went Waltzing Matilda through the Riverina, occasionally duffing (stealing) jumbucks (sheep) and usually camping under *Eucalyptus coolabah* that grows along rivers and billabongs, has often called this important matter into question. A billabong (billybung, incidentally, of the old-timers) is a backwater, not the river proper. At least one old balladist, J. P. Bourke, apostrophises his swag as a woman. In *My Swag and I* he sings:

> *But, ah! a wintry wind*
> *Awakes Matilda's charms*
> *I calmly spread the old girl out*
> *And snuggle in her arms.*

Neither does anybody seem certain of the derivation of the name of the great plain on which we were camped. It is generally assumed that the name is aboriginal, but the absence of trees over wide stretches might lead a Latinist to another view.

Next morning we found that we had slept within a couple of miles of the South Australian border. There is no gate. At the side of the road was a tall notice draped with an odd assortment of articles, on many of which were scrawled the names of James Smith, Mary Jones and other tourist travellers of the past.

It was at this camp that a car slowed down as it passed. It was driven by a gentleman with a reversed collar. Beside him sat the lady of some distant rectory and in the rear seat was our passenger of former days.

She waved gaily.

We argued for some time about the probable cause of her changed demeanour. Was it the result of the guarantee of a passage right across the desert? Could there have been a spiritual elevation brought about by improved associations? Perhaps it was because she had been pleasantly surprised by the contents of our envelope? Alas, we would never know.

Seventy miles on we called at Koonalda Station. A few miles beyond the station homestead is a great opening in the earth that we wanted to see. We were able to drive right to its edge. A pumping plant had once been installed to draw water up from the caves below. We climbed down ladders of iron piping to the rough and overgrown floor of a great pit. With electric torches we descended laterally into the darkness. It was a slippery climb over and around fallen limestone boulders. We reached a large cavern in which the beams of our torches were too feeble to reach the roof. Below us yawned another enormous pit. At the bottom of this lies a lake that you need a boat to explore. We had no equipment for further travels, and made our way back towards the sky. This was an interesting place, eerie with the distorted echoes of our voices rumbling through the darkness. There are almost certainly many caverns still undiscovered in the limestone. In the past aeroplanes have been used in attempts to find them. One aero club expedition used three co-operating planes and charted thirty-two chasms in a single operation. Some of these were subsequently investigated by land expeditions equipped with eighty foot rope-ladders and a small boat for use on the cool lakes hidden beneath the plain.

We called in at the Koonalda homestead on our way back to the road and met Mrs Gurney, her young children, and their pets. Twin young kangaroos – a rarity – hopped about the garden. There was also a great variety of birds. There were owls, and in one cage a big wedgetail eagle was recovering from a wing injury. Tame crows sat about the yard. A collection of stumpy-tailed lizards basked in the sun.

In the manner of bush children who do not often see strangers, these youngsters were shy at first, but on realising our interest in their pets they soon lost their shyness and took us on a tour of the zoo. These animals were the absorbing interest of their lives. Far removed from the entertainments and diversions of urban children, they derived joy and companionship from the creatures of the Nullarbor who became substitutes for the playmates that would be found in a more orthodox neighbourhood. We could not help contrasting the self-possessed attitude of these small people, once their initial shyness was overcome, and the fundamental knowledge they possessed, with that of the children of the towns. They are rich by comparison in the simplicities, if not the complexities, of life. Mrs Gurney teaches the children by means of correspondence courses. We told them to be sure to matriculate when perhaps, after university in Adelaide, a group of professional zoologists might rise out of the plain. We came away refreshed by this particular example of how some of the riches of life are not susceptible to entry into the ledgers of banks.

From Koonalda we headed through scrubby timber that gave way to open plains. The afternoon soon became hot, and there

Bush Children.   R.D. 61

Bush youngsters ... they are taught by correspondence courses.

was no wind. We stopped near a bore that supplied a small tank and trough. The run-off water had formed a small pond over which swallows were dipping and gathering mud for their nests on the sides of the tank. We pulled the truck alongside, and sitting within, set up cameras, for we knew that this isolated pool of water would attract other birds as well. The truck was a good hide and we had not long to wait before brilliant little scarlet cock chats began to arrive. These were quickly joined by the grey hens. From then on a variety of birds came to water. The most beautiful, perhaps, were two or three pairs of orange chats, lovely little creatures whose black and orange markings flashed in the sunlight as they and their red relatives flitted about the edges of the pond like tiny aristocrats among the more soberly dressed swallows. There were bush larks, too. We remained there for an hour or more, fascinated by this small scene of animation set in the vast flat plain.

It was nearing nightfall when we turned up the side track to Nullarbor Station. The wind had begun to rise again, and the evening sky to the west was streaked with high flying trails of wispy cloud. We were made welcome at the station, and offered quarters in a hut where there was firewood and a cooking place. It did not take long to get a fire going. We took our swags into the hut and laid them out on plain stretcher beds. We spent a good night out of reach of the cutting wind. Before dawn the wind died, and a heavy mist like a sea-fog blanketed the plain. It was shivery cold and the water felt icy as we sluiced our faces from the tank. We now had to leave the main east-west road for the Maralinga bomb-range. After breakfast, we got directions along the lonely track that runs north through the saltbush to the Transcontinental Railway line about eighty miles north.

Typical of bush hospitality we were given some loaves of fresh bread. Many times we were to reflect how much in the Australian outback hospitality to a stranger is a natural reaction, never a studied grace.

A few miles out we felt almost as though we were at sea. From the roof of the truck we could see nothing but the plain. It reached to the horizon all about us. It was covered with saltbush except for the places that were carpeted with daisies. The track was merely wheel marks that wound around and about broken slabs of limestone. In the deeper pockets of topsoil, wombats had excavated burrows like giant foxes' earths. Obviously, they are very common. The few scattered people of the Nullarbor hunt these blunt-ended marsupials and cure them for bacon. We were told that wombat ham is very good. There are other ways of cooking them. One young fellow had told us that it was a pity we were not staying longer.

'You ought to taste Mum's wombat stew,' he said.

The explorer Flinders said that the flesh of wombat 'resembles lean mutton in taste, and to us was acceptable food'. Flinders saw clearly its relationship to the amiable though dull-witted koala, which is essentially a wombat, the ancestors of which took to the trees. 'Another species of this animal has been discovered in New South Wales, which lives in the tops of trees and, in manners, bears much resemblance to the sloth.'[1]

Today very few people hunt wombats except in the places where they are so plentiful that they break down fences or burrow beneath dirt roads and cause them to cave in under heavy traffic. They are harmless vegetarians, square and purposeful, and of a benign disposition and unruffled equanimity. The explorer, Bass, describing a wombat in the 1790's wrote of it as 'an animal of quiet mien, most economically made'. The wombat is a creature that would have delighted Edward Lear. It is easily tamed and, in an undemonstrative way, capable of affection. But it makes an unsuitable pet, for it is nocturnal in its habits. By day it becomes exceedingly sleepy, though when awakened it sometimes indulges in a certain ponderous playfulness. Then it will suddenly fall again into a heavy sleep. If you pick up a wild wombat in both arms he may submit with a resigned air. However, his jaws are powerful and he may reach out casually and grasp your arm in a rather tight hold. He tends to do this without ferocity, but in a seemingly thoughtful manner. It takes quite a little persuasion before he will relinquish his grip.

We came to an abandoned well. The heap of spoil from the digging consisted of broken limestone that was full of fossil shells. Three or four feet below the surface of the well, on a ledge of rock, sat two young kestrels regarding us fearfully. The sun was shining directly on them and they made ideal targets for our cameras. Then, just after midday, Tim, who was driving, suddenly pointed ahead.

'What on earth is that?'

Looking through the windscreen we saw what happened to be a series of thin, gleaming white towers reaching high into the

[1] Some zoologists now believe wombats and the koala are only very remotely related.

sky. Clearly these must be a mirage, but they were like no mirage any of us had ever seen.

After another half an hour's driving the towers began to diminish. Then we realised that the mirage had distorted into great elongations a group of small wooden fettlers' huts at the railway camp at Fisher, one of several such situated along the Transcontinental Line. There was a bore, and a watering tower for locomotives. We found neat rows of white painted huts facing the line. In front of one or two of these were small gardens, bravely defying the alien landscape. There was no one in sight.

We went over to a couple of the huts. They were empty, and we realised that the men who lived in them must be out on their maintenance work somewhere up along the line. We pulled into the shade of the water-tank beside the rails. In this treeless area firewood is scarce, but soon we scrounged a few sticks and boiled the billy. The rails stretched away in a dead straight line in either direction. They were supported by crushed limestone rock, rich with fossils. A railway ballasted with the rubbish of a sea that existed 12 million years ago.

Behind each cottage stood a kind of sentry box. On investigation, these were found to contain stocks of magazines. This was too much for some of us who retired to the comfort of these monuments of hygiene for a quiet and contemplative moment. Silence reigned in the drowsy heat of noon.

This silence was broken by an ear-splitting whistle that cut the air like a rocket. Incredibly, out of the mirage appeared a train. A great monster of a thing, it resolved itself into a huge diesel engine pulling two or three coaches and a long string of flat-cars loaded with bright new motor cars for Kalgoorlie and Perth. The train slowly slid to a smooth halt and a half-Chinese guard jumped down and approached the one of us who stood there staring as if it were the first train he had ever seen.

'Where'll I put the stuff – in the usual possie?'

As the guard ask the question he hauled out sacks of bread, mail and parcels.

'Yair – the usual possie.'

There seemed no other answer.

From the windows of the carriages a couple of passengers watched as the guard stowed the packages into a small hut along-side the line. Behind the cottages two half-opened doors revealed two astonished faces. Here, in the middle of this wilderness, the sudden and silent approach of the train came as a complete surprise. Although we knew that trains must in fact frequently run along the line, we somehow never expected to see one. It seemed too remote, too far removed from anywhere for anything so mundane.

'You right now, mate? Nothing you want passed on?' the half-Chinese guard said.

'She's right, thanks. Nothing to pass on.'

'O.K. Be seeing you, mate,' the guard said.

He stepped away from the train and waved his arm. The engine screamed a whistle. Climbing up the step, the guard nodded briefly as his van began to slide away. It seemed to take a long time before the mirage swallowed the big train and its glittering cargo of motor cars. There was no sound, for the great space of the plain absorbed the thudding of the diesel.

We were all startled by the sudden brief appearance of this symbol of bustling energy, and the train crew's nonchalant acceptance of ourselves as normal furnishing of the plain. In a curious way the whole episode had the quality of a dream. Out of silence and mirage, incomprehensible forms resolve themselves unexpectedly into the familiar, and as quickly dissolve again in the void of space. Perhaps we will never again see huts or a train as clearly in the mind as we did that day.

From this little settlement we set out along a rough track strewn with slabs of limestone towards the small township of Watson, fifty miles to the eastward. Here we had to report to a security officer before moving north to the Maralinga bomb-range. Twenty miles along the line we met four fettlers on a motor-driven trolley. They were the Fisher gang. We told them something they already knew; that their bread and mail had been delivered. We stayed yarning for some time. They seemed to enjoy the chance to talk. One of them was a Yorkshireman, another a Swede, one was from Adelaide and the youngest was a sun-tanned lad from Newtown, Sydney. When he found that we were from the big town he asked nostalgically for news for, he said, he'd been out on the line for nearly a year. But we couldn't give him much, explaining that none of us had seen the place for some time either. They all said they liked the life on the line and that here they really could save money. There was simply nowhere to spend it.

We talked a lot about the post-war peopling of Australia and the characteristics of the various types of immigrants as we bumped over the plain alongside the railway. A Yorky, a Swede and a couple of Australians working together out in the Never-Never. We had seen the same sort of thing in many places. This new, multi-tribal intermingling is the result of a purposeful post-war migration policy, and is allowed by the prosperity of a young nation exploding into activity.

For example, in April 1960 they began to dig the foundations, and landscape the gardens, for the new Monash University.[1] By March 1961 there were completed enough permanent lecture theatres and laboratories to enable the staff to begin teaching the first 350 of an ultimate 12,000 odd students in the faculties of Arts, Economics, Medicine, Science and Engineering.

A babel of languages still floats from new trenches and scaffolds. Students with names such as Bottomley, Eustace and Higginbotham; Ingwersen, Muhlen-Schulte and Zidek; Sin Pee Liew, Boh Ghee Yap and Guan Chock Chong, alias King Sock (who are there on visitors' scholarships), began their professional careers under teachers from Manchester, Melbourne, Oxford, Cambridge, Sydney, London, Perth, Liverpool, Otago, Brisbane, Sheffield and Hungary. This pattern of internationality is being repeated in construction and other projects all over the continent.

Of all the migrants, the British are generally held to be the most desirable. Although they bring with them fewer 'new' skills than do the Continentals, they do not form 'racial' groups. They make up more than half the new-comers and, in fact, Australia currently receives more British migrants than any other dominion. Britons are more popular in Australia than they are in Africa and the Orient where they tend to get a bit above themselves in their dealings with 'the natives'. In Australia, on the other hand, the southern English in particular seem often to become a little pathetic. In a country of detached houses and gardens, many tend to pine for Mrs Brown on the terrace steps next door, and for the daily escape diet of *minutiae* concerning the public – and alas, private – lives of Royalty on which they were fed by the British press. They seem particularly distressed, too, by the absence of free medical, dental and prescription services. The British national pastime of 'grousing' (to use an English phrase) has given rise in Australia to the derisive expression *wingeing*

[1] Named after General Sir John Monash (1865-1931), probably the greatest Jewish general since Joshua. A graduate in engineering, arts and law, Monash was an amateur soldier who rose to command the Australian Corps in the First World War. His culminating military triumph was the piercing of the Hindenburg Line in the autumn of 1918.

pommy. (In colonial days the highly-coloured complexions of many Englishmen caused them to be called pomegranates, a play on 'immigrants'. This was soon abbreviated to 'pommy', a term that may be affectionate or otherwise according to the preceding adjective and the tone in which it is used.)

Pommies of north-country, or other extra-southern origin, almost invariably earn more respect than those from the south. They are, in biological terminology, to some degree *preadapted* to the Australian atmosphere of egalitarianism and comparative candour. The difference in outlook between the Australian and Englishman is very clearly seen in their respective social attitudes when visiting each other's country. The Australian usually has something to say about the beauty and squalor of England, the high scholarship of a number and the peasant-like ignorance of many, the dirty surgeries of some and the fastidious professional standards of others; and about the almost universal disinclination of the educated classes to distinguish between manners and principles. He looks at the B.B.C. television programmes, and is frank in his comparison of their quality with the poor syndicated stuff to which he is accustomed at home. He is enthralled by English architecture up to and including the Regency; but he is not without an opinion on the local tribal customs responsible for the sickening instances of child cruelty, and the weirdly high incidence of socially feminised males that he sees reported in the London press. He may say a great deal, but he rarely thinks it worthwhile to commit his criticisms to print.

The English visitor to Australia, on the other hand, tends to be fulsome in his praise of almost everything he sees. But often there are unspoken thoughts lurking behind southern English eyes, and these are transferred to a metaphorical little black book a bit further back still. Later, he tends to write the nasty little things that he failed to mention while among the people whose hospitality he accepted. This unlovable trait has led to the application of the expression *kipper* to a certain type of Englishman. A kipper, by virtue of its processing, has become two-faced with no guts. When Australian friends read his printed statements they are usually a little shocked.

'There's a lot in what he says,' they mutter disappointedly, 'but why didn't the dear fellow say it when he was with us?'

Notwithstanding the shortcomings of the kipper-type Briton, it is nevertheless probably true to say that, among the big national groups, the British are the most welcome. They assimilate so well.

Usually they, and almost always their children, come to identify themselves completely with the new land. It is good to see a first generation lad of British parents threshing along in an exhausting surf-race, or slugging it out in the fifth set, on level terms with the others. Sport success, once the techniques are mastered and the hard training is behind, is much a matter of the mind. In his new egalitarian environment, the migrant's child feels as good as the best of them and his performance is raised correspondingly. He is learning the national philosophy of 'give it a go' and is ready 'to declare the other fellow on'. When he comes up against his British cousin at the Olympic or Empire Games, on the tennis court, or even on the cricket field,[1] he will generally win.

The native Englishman has no such comfortable feeling of confidence. From earliest childhood he is taught to know his 'place' both in regard to Royalty and the Establishment at the apex of his local society, and the innominate herd at the base of the triangle. By and large, he accepts his 'station', his place in peck-order. When confronted by an authoritative thick-legged or green-capped 'Aussie', or a crew-cut 'Yank', or a stadium full of bawling whistling Latins, his confidence tends to ooze away. A socially conditioned tendency to compromise in the face of *authority* manifests itself. The result of this social inferiority can be counted in the respective number of gold medals won by Australian and Britons at successive Olympiads. Though they often ascribe an 'inferiority complex' to 'Yanks', 'Huns', Latins, 'colonials' and others, the British seem strangely blind to its stultifying existence among themselves. Yet it emerges starkly in all kinds of curious ways. It is manifest in compensatory over-statements such as 'British is Best', 'Britain Stood Alone', and 'Britain (or Churchill) Saved the World'. This nonsense tends to bore people whom experience has forced changes to American, German, or local products, and particularly those with kinsmen buried in Greece, Crete, the Western Desert and elsewhere.

An explanation of this, recently hypertrophied, British sensitivity is that the process of growing down in the world is rather

[1] Contrary to popular belief, Australians are relatively little interested in the game of cricket. Their chief sports are sea-swimming and tennis and, in the southern parts of the continent, Australian Rules football. There is insufficient interest in cricket to support a single full-time professional. Australians are Saturday afternoon cricketers except during the annual inter-state matches, and, logically, should never beat an English test team. It is only during international matches that cricket has great spectator appeal there.

more painful than that of growing up. A few years ago a North American food importer announced to the press that he preferred the strawberry jam of old England to that of his own country. (He was probably right, too.)

'Our Jam Best,' chorused the mass-circulation London dailies. 'British Jam. Superior Qualities Praised,' announced *The Times*.

When this crashing inferiority makes it impossible for English sporting reporters to admit that a British team is ever beaten fairly, the matter becomes less amusing because they do the United Kingdom immeasurable harm abroad. Such writers and broadcasters glibly give it out that a Briton prefers to be a 'good loser'; or that really, he was denied proper training facilities; or was beaten by the heat, or the cold; or that the other chaps didn't bowl, but threw the ball; or the track was bad; or the crowd was too partisan; or it was the fault of the referee or umpire. The English sporting journalist, 'armed with powerful field glasses', generally knows better than the umpire whether the chap is 'out' or not. These unworthy whines, sent to Britain for ego-lifting home consumption, are immediately cabled back across the world where they are read by the sporting crowd who saw the match, and know what really happened. Australians have written sardonically to newspapers urging that cricket umpires should be removed from near the wickets. It would be better, it has been argued, that umpires should be put 250 yards away in the press box, 'armed with powerful field glasses'.

It must be emphasised that such compensatory excuses rarely emanate from the British athletes or games players. Almost alone it is their press representatives who have earned the British an international reputation as a nation of squealers in the very countries – North America, Europe, India and Australia – where they are most trying to make friends. It is very sad. And unnecessary, too.

16

We bumped along beside the railway to Watson, a tiny township of several houses, and a Commonwealth Police Office to which we reported. The work on which we were engaged at Maralinga has no place in this story. We spent some time at the base where we slept in sheets, went to motion pictures whenever we wanted to, ate ridiculously good food and used base facilities to overhaul the truck.

Then we started on the last stages of the journey home. But before leaving Watson we spent some hours in a quarry there. This quarry supplies limestone ballast for the railway line. It is about sixty feet deep, and its exposed rubble is packed with Miocene fossils. The place was fascinating but the sun's heat reflected from the rocks converted the quarry into something like a furnace. After a couple of hours collecting we called it a day and set out east along the line for Ooldea.

This is another fettlers' settlement, where some of the men live with their families. But Ooldea is far more than this, for it will always be remembered as the lonely place where an indomitable Irishwoman, Mrs Daisy Bates, spent sixteen years amongst nomad tribesmen, tending the old, and the very young, and those who were sick. Altogether, *Kabali* (or grandmother) as she was called, spent thirty-five years of her life in the service of the aborigines.

Daisy Bates came from Tipperary. She was young Miss O'Dwyer-Hunt when a tendency to phthisis caused her to visit Australia in 1884. After a while she went back to England and joined the staff of *The Times* at a salary of £1 per week in the day of Wickham Steed. When it was alleged that the aborigines were being abominably treated in Western Australia, she came back as special correspondent. She reported that the brown people were not, in fact, ill-treated, but were mismanaged. While in Australia she married a cattleman, James Bates, who died and left her 183,600 acres in central Western Australia. These she sold. Thereafter she used her life and money for the benefit of the aborigines. She never gave up her Edwardian dress. She wore an ankle-length black skirt, a white blouse with a prim high collar, a silk ribbon tie and a fly veil. She carried a black umbrella. In the great spaces of this semi-desert land she presented a remarkable appearance. On her rare trips into cities she declined to use escalators or motor cars. She did not listen to the wireless, nor would she enter a cinema. Ill health made her retire to Adelaide in 1945 where she lived until her death six years later.

At Ooldea we saw her small stone memorial on which is fixed a bronze bas-relief. This depicts the image of Daisy Bates, and those of the people she loved. It stands alone beneath a small group of acacias, not far from the line, a lonely and moving reminder of a life of devoted service to an ancient and primitive people whose tribal ways were broken and disrupted by the coming of the European.

We crossed the line once more, and headed south along a narrow, rough trail that would bring us, a hundred miles later, to the main east-west road. At first the plain was treeless. Then clumps of acacias began to appear, and when we camped about forty miles south of Ooldea we had ample firewood again. We disturbed a brown hawk that had made a late kill of a rabbit. It made off reluctantly as we came up. The sky was the colour of deep rose from the dying sun. But, as usual, the wind began to rise, and we were glad to pull our swags close about the fire.

Next day, the track wound through sandy country. Sometimes we crossed salt-pans. As the day wore on trees became more profuse and, as we passed Colona Station homestead at the junction of the main road, we ran once more through tall trees and mallee scrub, indicating our approach to the Eyre Peninsula, the Nullarbor's end. From now on we would come to small townships and a developing wheat country. We now knew that soon the wide, unfenced land through which we had travelled for so long would be left behind. We saw the Port Lincoln parrots perched among the trees about the camp in the light of the early morning sun. The colour of these birds flashed and shimmered in the dawn light as they squabbled in the branches above us. There were thousands of budgerygahs; they nested in the broken hollow tree spouts above our camps and sailed in undulating flocks across the plain. It was an engrossing thought that these would fetch thirty bob a pair in Tooting; and that the Cheam and Pinner people might give that price, too.

Again the nights were cold, but we had good fires of mallee roots. These throw out great heat before burning away to a white ash. At Ceduna there was no mail. We did not linger. From Port Augusta we ran on bitumen, once more back in closely settled country. These lands were rich and green to eyes that had become accustomed to the dry of the west. The great growth of a flowering weed, Salvation Jane, covered the hillsides with a startling purple and green.

It was strange, and not altogether convenient, to find ourselves back again in closely settled country. After months in the great spaces we had the mild feeling of being shut in. Previously we camped wherever we wished; now we found ourselves held to the road by fences. Sometimes it was not easy to find a good camp quickly, nor to find big logs for the fire. There seemed to be a ridiculously large number of farm-houses and small towns. After spending weeks away from people we always suffer this reaction. We disapproved of so many people. Traffic was bothersome. Everybody seemed to be in a hurry. Cars were unnecessarily flashy to eyes grown accustomed to trucks and jeeps, and they appeared to be driven by maniacs. When we pulled up by the road nobody stopped to see if we were all right nor even just to have a yarn. We were quickly becoming used to a different way of life and a different tempo. Here tomorrow meant tomorrow. Time had again become a matter of hours or even minutes; not of sun-up or dusk, or days or weeks. *People whom we had never met before, and from whom we asked directions, talked to us as though we were strangers.*

This was strange, but soon we slipped back into what seemed abnormality and, as we pounded past a hideous new Adelaide housing estate called (of course) Elizabeth, we thought of the track as one might recall a dream.

17

Now we were at the gateway of the wowser belt. A wowser is a gentleman who uses a contraceptive as a book-mark for his Bible. Adelaide, and its larger south-eastern neighbour Melbourne, are traditionally the wowser cities, although Melbourne has reputedly a higher crime rate than Sydney, her sophisticated, and supposedly naughtier, northern sister. Adelaide and Melbourne both have a reputation for the repression of any books that may, from time to time, excite the disapproval of the small, but vociferous wowser groups that flourish there. There are in the Australian provinces no watch committees such as pester the sweet sherry belt of England. Nevertheless, there are little coveys of wowsers, and the wowsers of Adelaide and Melbourne exert an influence that is entirely disproportionate to the numbers of people whom they manage to attract to their churches.

In these cities laymen as well as professional *sin-shifters* still write rhetorical letters to metropolitan newspapers condemning 'devotees of the fallacious doctrine of evolution' whenever a review of an 'overseas' (a much used expression) book gives them opportunity to do so. Quicker than you can say *Darwin!* these earnest men cite in their support the opinions of 19th century 'authorities' such as Herbert Spencer, not to mention those of the late Mr George Bernard Shaw. In these cities, newspaper editors who have worked previously in a wider world will, in compliance with local custom, cynically grant up to half a column of space to a single such Edwardian incongruity.

South Australia and Victoria are the only Australian states in which it is illegal to serve an intoxicating drink (unless accompanied by a meal) after 6 p.m. It is a special dispensation of the Almighty that any organic matter can be fermented to produce spirituous liquors and, ironically, the grapes of South Australia and north-western Victoria produce some of the best light wines fermented by God and man. Yet, until recently, if you were taking a bottle with your meal in an Adelaide or Melbourne restaurant, along came a little man at 8 p.m. and whisked it right from under your palate. It was legal then, to take sherry with soup, but criminal to open a bottle of claret with the entree. Even tonight they will whip the bottle off the table at 10 o'clock.

Quaintly, Melbournians seem to relish the thorn they have strapped to their sides, along with the trams that still clank heavily about their city. On several occasions their state government has given them the opportunity by referendum to extend the drinking hours. Each time a majority of the citizens has voted to retain 6 o'clock closing. It is the women's vote, they say, that defeats successive proposals for extension. The suburban and country Mum want Dad home for 'tea' i.e. dinner. Sophisticated Melbournians say, a trifle maliciously and perhaps fallaciously, that in their last referendum only two large areas voted for an extension of licensing hours that would bring the state of Victoria into line with Queensland, New South Wales, Western Australia, Tasmania and Northern Territory. These two places, they say, are the more exclusive residential areas on the one hand, and the heavily industrial, on the other. The Toorak and neighbouring types are travelled, and reasonably educated people and they voted to let themselves and others drink at any times that seemed sensible. The industrialists, so to speak, reputedly told their wives to vote for late closing or they would strike them heavily with pick-handles.[1]

The worthy wowsers of Adelaide have never allowed the rest of the populace to state their views by means of a referendum.[2]

In both Adelaide and Melbourne, vice squads of policemen of

[1] Times have changed since this was first written. The Bolte Government has gone over the heads of the wowsers and brought Victorian drinking laws into line with those of the more advanced States.

[2] But in September 1967, South Australia's new Premier, Mr Dunstan, amended the law following a Royal Commission.

varying degrees of literacy have legal power to descend on book-sellers who have in stock literature that the wowsers have told the police is improper. It matters not that the Commonwealth Literary Board in Canberra (which exercises powers broadly comparable with those of the Lord Chamberlain in Britain) has already granted a book unrestricted entry into the Commonwealth.

'Eh, Jack, here's one by this red bloke Burns!' shouted a foraging policeman, his hand on the shoulder of one particular volume.

'Burns?'

'Yair! *The Political Works of Robert Burns.*'

He waved the book exultantly.

When a scientist was equipping a department of a new university near Melbourne he was given a series of anatomical specimens by his English colleagues. These were packed with a couple of teaching films and consigned to Melbourne. The packing case was marked 'Scientific Materials'.

It was opened by a university employee at the request of local customs officials. Two circular cannisters glistened wickedly among innocent bones.

'*Films!*'

Visions of all kinds of delectable nastiness rose before official eyes.

The startled import clerk tried to explain that the cannisters doubtless contained educational films, and that the Foundation Professor of Biology was extremely unlikely to import pornography under university seal. To no avail. The films were whisked away into a dark-room and quickly projected. Alas, the officers had a dull forty minutes peering at the internal anatomy of *Periplaneta*, the cockroach, and *Lumbricus*, the earthworm. The only beastliness in the film were a couple of conjugating single-celled *Paramœceum*, but the chaps did not understand what this was about.

But all Adelaidians are not wowsers and it was good indeed to see old friends again. We luxuriated in baths, good food and clean clothes. We devoured newspapers and magazines, and in a few days lost the sense of the simplicity of camp life. Small things like shaving every day, the pleasure of wine with meals, and a haircut, restored us to former living. Yet, when we left Adelaide to travel across the south-eastern corner to Sydney, we again camped for a few nights and slipped quickly back into the routine of the last few months.

18

The last run home was by way of Canberra, leading us across the western plains of New South Wales. It is in this part of Australia that a large proportion of the nation's wool clip is grown. Yet it is so wide and broad that one may drive all day and see very few sheep. These are classical grounds: it was in this country that the national ethos of the outback and the romantic conception of the bushman had its beginnings and came to something like maturity after the gold-rushes. From 1815, when the way across the Great Divide was found from Sydney Town, the explorers, and next the land-takers and the bush workers, pushed further and further into the hinterland. The land-takers, legally and otherwise, 'squatted' and established sheep-runs. Here the camaraderie and hospitality of the bush was established. The bush ballads began to evolve. Soon, in the mid-century, came the first real gold-rushes, and a swift influx of adventurers from all over the world.

When the gold had 'cut out', more and more people took up vacant land. But a big proportion of the restless gold miners remained nomads. They and later their sons moved from station to station, tank-sinking, timber-splitting, shearing, boundary-riding and droving.

I had written him a letter which I had, for want of better
Knowledge, sent to where I met him down the Lachlan, years ago,
He was shearing when I knew him, so I sent the letter to him,
Just 'on spec' addressed as follows: 'Clancy, of the Overflow'.
And an answer came directed in a writing unexpected,
(And I think the same was written with a thumb-nail dipped in tar).
'Twas his shearing mate who wrote it, and verbatim I will quote it:
'Clancy's gone to Queensland droving, and we don't know where he are.'

From these men there emerged a distinct social group and a way of life. The freedom and the independence that it created in the individual gave to them an air of adventure and romance.

There was movement at the station, for the word had passed around
That the colt from old Regret had got away,
And had joined the wild bush horses – he was worth a thousand pound,
So all the cracks had gathered to the fray.
All the tried and noted riders from the stations near and far
Had mustered at the homestead overnight . . .

They found the horses by a big clump of wattles and the mob, including the thoroughbred, raced away into the ranges.

Then fast the horsemen followed, where the gorges deep and black
Resounded to the thunder of their tread,
And the stockwhips woke the echoes, and they fiercely answered back
From cliffs and crags that beetled overhead.
And upward, ever upward, the wild horses held their way,
Where mountain ash and kurrajong grew wide;
And the old man muttered fiercely, 'We may bid the mob good-day,
'No man can hold them down the other side.'

But the man from Snowy River galloped his stock-horse down

the mountainside full of fallen logs, wild hop scrub and wombat holes. He chased the mob through the ranges and 'alone and unassisted brought them back'.

> *But his hardy mountain pony he could scarcely raise a trot,*
> *He was blood from hip to shoulder from the spur;*
> *But his pluck was still undaunted, and his courage fiery hot,*
> *For never yet was mountain horse a cur.*
> *And down by Kosciusko, where the pine-clad ridges raise*
> *Their torn and rugged battlements on high,*
> *Where the air is clear as crystal, and the white stars fairly blaze*
> *At midnight in the cold and frosty sky,*
> *And where around the Overflow the reed-beds sweep and sway*
> *To the breezes, and the rolling plains are wide,*
> *The man from Snowy River is a household word today,*
> *And the stockmen tell the story of his ride.*

In Victorian days, it was fashionable for the Currency Lads, the native-born of Sydney and Melbourne, to imitate the dress and mannerisms of the bushmen. The legends of derring do, of cattle duffing and bushrangers, helped build this ethos and the bush songs and ballads that were increasingly derived from it.

In recent years, the memories and the legends have been debased by grotesque little men with Hawaiian steel guitars and big Hollywood hats who wail the old songs, and some new ones, in voices resembling that of a badly-cut bull calf. They may even yodel. To these, our children listen with an obvious and horrible relish. We are growing old.

Our last camp was near the bank of the Murrumbidgee out beyond Hay. The plain is open grassland, but along the banks of the river grow tall flood gums. Some drovers we met advised us to camp back from the river in the open unless we wanted to be eaten alive by mosquitoes.

'Big bastards, like wasps,' we were told they were.

They were not as big as wasps but we moved back just the same. We were in a large sheep reserve, government land held free for the use of drovers and their travelling flocks. Half a mile away from us a mob of two or three thousand sheep was camped down for the night. We could see the light of the drovers' fire twinkling in the distance. There was a spectacular sunset over the plain that night. It left the darkening sky a rich translucent blue and the evening star shone with a pure white light.

FINIS

Journey Among Men The Maps

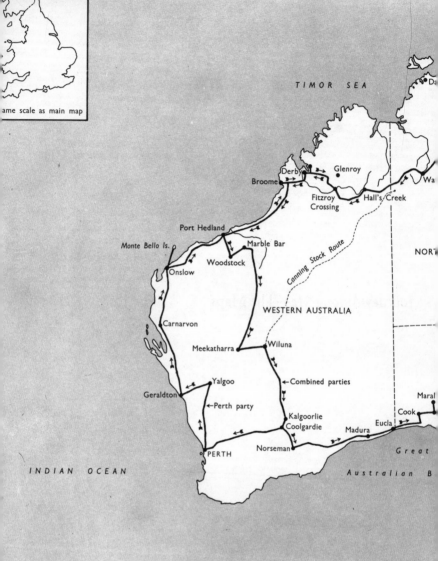

same scale as main map

TIMOR SEA

Da

Glenroy

Derby

Broome

Fitzroy
Crossing   Hall's Creek   Wa

Port Hedland

Monte Bello Is. ○   Marble Bar

Woodstock

Onslow   NOR

Carnarvon   WESTERN AUSTRALIA

Canning Stock Route

Meekatharra   Wiluna

Yalgoo   ← Combined parties   Maral

Geraldton   Cook

← Perth party   Kalgoorlie   Eucla
                    Coolgardie   Madura

PERTH   Norseman   Great

INDIAN OCEAN   Australian B

APPROXIMATE SCALE—MILES

0   250   500

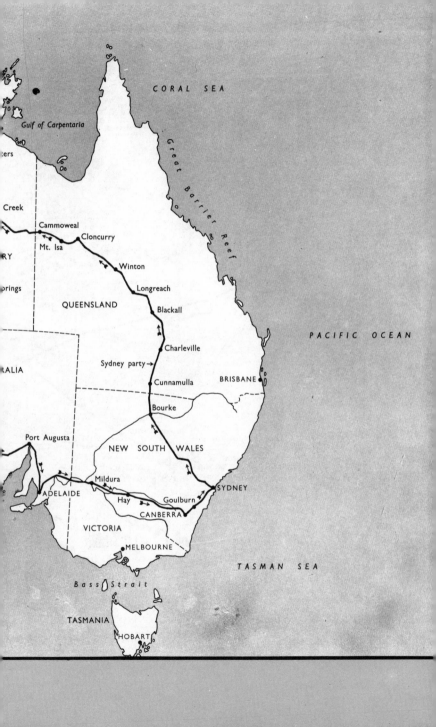

Index